Amman

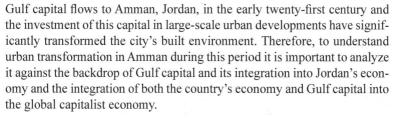

Gulf capital flows to Amman, Jordan, in the early twenty-first century and the investment of this capital in large-scale urban developments have significantly transformed the city's built environment. Therefore, to understand urban transformation in Amman during this period it is important to analyze it against the backdrop of Gulf capital and its integration into Jordan's economy and the integration of both the country's economy and Gulf capital into the global capitalist economy.

This book analyzes three cases of megaprojects planned for the city in the early twenty-first century: The New Downtown (Abdali), Jordan Gate, and Sanaya Amman. Drawing upon theories on urban development and capitalism, identity, and discourse, and urban development processes and cases in other cities, the book investigates how contemporary megaprojects in Amman fit into the capitalist economy and its modes of production, how capital flows construct a modern image of the city, and how the new image and megaprojects represent the city residents as modern and create Amman as a global city.

This book presents a new approach to the study of the urban built environment in Amman, providing a valuable interdisciplinary contribution to the scholarly work on globalizing cities, especially in the Middle East.

Majd Musa holds a PhD in architecture from the University of Illinois at Urbana-Champaign, USA. She is an assistant professor of architecture at the University of Sharjah, United Arab Emirates. Her research interest is contemporary architecture and urbanism with a focus on globalizing Middle Eastern cities.

Built Environment City Studies

Seville: Through the Urban Void
Miguel Torres

Amman: Gulf Capital, Identity, and Contemporary Megaprojects
Majd Musa

Amman

Gulf Capital, Identity, and Contemporary Megaprojects

Majd Musa

LONDON AND NEW YORK

First published 2017
by Routledge
2 Park Square, Milton Park, Abingdon, Oxon OX14 4RN

and by Routledge
711 Third Avenue, New York, NY 10017

First issued in paperback 2018

Routledge is an imprint of the Taylor & Francis Group, an informa business

British Library Cataloguing-in-Publication Data
A catalogue record for this book is available from the British Library

Library of Congress Cataloging-in-Publication Data
Names: Musa, Majd, author.
Title: Amman : Gulf capital, identity, and contemporary megaprojects /
    Majd Musa.
Description: Milton Park, Abingdon, Oxon ; New York, NY :
    Routledge, 2017. | Series: Built Environment City Studies |
    Includes bibliographical references and index.
Identifiers: LCCN 2016046571 | ISBN 9781138679078 (hardback :
    alk. paper) | ISBN 9781315558585 (ebook)
Subjects: LCSH: Urbanization—Jordan—Amman. | Globalization—
    Jordan—Amman.
Classification: LCC HT147.J6 M87 2017 | DDC 307.76—dc23
LC record available at https://lccn.loc.gov/2016046571

ISBN 13: 978-1-138-34201-9 (pbk)
ISBN 13: 978-1-138-67907-8 (hbk)

Typeset in Times New Roman
by Apex CoVantage, LLC

In Memory of My Parents

Contents

Figures

Preface

Having lived in Amman, Jordan, for a good part of the first decade of the twenty-first century, I had the chance to witness firsthand the construction boom in the city during that time. It was obvious to me as an architect and researcher that this unprecedented urban change in the city was unlikely to be understood as a local or national phenomenon. The images of the new developments on billboards and construction fence signs and banners, the names of the developers, and sometimes the names of the developments all reminded me of what I had experienced in the UAE where I had lived before moving to Jordan. What exactly was the connection between urban development in Amman and UAE cities, as well as other Arab Gulf cities? How and why was this connection made possible? It was not before I started my PhD studies in architecture at the University of Illinois at Urbana-Champaign, USA, that I began to find answers to these questions and make sense of the new urban transformation in Amman. Reflecting on theories and understandings I learned in Prof. John Stallmeyer's class on globalization and its influences on urban and architectural production, I began to realize that Amman was being created as a competitive global city, not least through the production of contemporary megaprojects that were made possible through capital flows to the city, primarily from the Gulf. This would years later become the topic of the current book.

Much of the research in this book was carried out as a part of my PhD dissertation, which I completed in 2013 at the University of Illinois at Urbana-Champaign, USA. I am thankful to the Fulbright program for supporting the first two years of my studies there. Also I benefited from several fellowships at Illinois: Alan K. and Leonarda F. Laing Memorial Fellowship, Ernest L. and Reba E. Stouffer Fellowship, and University Fellowship. Thanks to all faculty and staff at the University of Illinois who impressed me with their professionalism and made my experience at Illinois rewarding. I am especially grateful to my dissertation advisor Prof. John Stallmeyer for his continuous support, insightful discussions, and valuable input throughout my work on the dissertation. Thanks to professors D. Fairchild Ruggles, Lynne Dearborn, and Kenneth Cuno for their guidance and thoughtful comments on the drafts of my dissertation.

Thanks to officials at Greater Amman Municipality and National Resources Investment & Development Corporation (Mawared) who were willing to help. Thanks to Abdali Investment and Development (AID), LACECO, and Consolidated Consultants – Jafar Tukan Architects who provided some of the materials on the study cases and offered me interviews. I am especially grateful to the late Jafar Tukan for his cooperation, kindness, and hospitality. Criticism of projects developed or designed by any of these institutions, corporations, firms, or individuals should in no way detract from my respect for and gratitude to them.

Thanks to the research participants in Amman for their valuable contributions. Thanks to architects Rasem Badran, Ayman Zuaiter, and Ismail Tahhan who allowed me to interview them and shared with me their views and ideas about recent transformation in Amman's built environment. Thanks to my previous colleagues at the Center for the Study of the Built Environment (CSBE) for their support. I am grateful to Prof. Mohammad al-Asad with whom I had the great pleasure to study, work, and write and from whom I learned a lot.

Thanks to my publisher Routledge/Taylor and Francis, particularly Sadé Lee for her continuous support throughout the writing process. Thanks to Louise Baird-Smith for being very helpful at the stage of preparing and approving the proposal of this book. Thanks to May Musa, Nora Eltayeib, and my publisher for helping with the illustrations in this book, and thanks to May also for keeping me updated on the latest developments in Amman.

At the University of Sharjah, I am especially grateful to Prof. Mohamed Maalej, Acting Dean of the College of Engineering, for his continuous support and encouragement. I am also thankful to the colleagues who supported me in the past couple of years. Thanks to my lovely students for the interesting discussions inside and outside the classroom.

I will always be indebted to my late parents for all the love and help that they provided. I am blessed to have Maha, Ghassan, May, and Bassam as my siblings. They have always been there for me and kept pushing me to finish this work. It is difficult to find words that adequately express my appreciation and love.

1 Introduction

Globalization processes, including the flows of capital, goods, people, technology, and information, have been increasingly transforming cities, and countries, over the past few decades in ways unprecedented in intensity or extensity. The Jordanian capital, Amman, is no exception. Since the mid-twentieth century and particularly in the early twenty-first century, Amman has been undergoing significant economic, political, social, and cultural changes and dramatic physical transformations at the architectural and urban scales. Today, a "global"[1] Amman is in the making: mixed-use megaprojects, high-end high-rise buildings, gated communities, and large-scale designer shopping malls have become a dominant form of architectural and urban production in the city.[2] These dramatic transformations in Amman's urban built environment are influenced by interrelated global, regional, national, and local economic, political, social, and cultural forces. However, the most significant force of transformation in the built environment of Amman in the early twenty-first century was Gulf capital flows and their investment in urban developments in the city. During most of the 2000s, oil prices increased significantly. Because oil constituted a major part of the capital of oil-exporting Arab Gulf states (Bahrain, Kuwait, Oman, Qatar, Saudi Arabia, and United Arab Emirates), the economy of these states witnessed significant growth. In addition, Gulf states had by then diversified their economy to include sovereign wealth funds and state- and privately owned foreign assets and equities, further enhancing their global economic integration.[3] As a result during this period, these states had surpluses of current accounts, which they exported as capital to be invested in Middle Eastern and North African states, including Jordan, in industries, banking, telecommunications, tourism, and real estate development (see Hanieh, 2011, 2013; Oxford Business Group [OBG], 2008; Pfeifer, 2010). Gulf capital flows led to a vigorous construction boom in Amman and other Jordanian cities during most of the 2000s. That construction boom came to an end in the late 2000s as the effects of the 2008 global economic crisis influenced the Gulf economy and began to affect Jordan. In the early 2010s, as oil prices and Gulf foreign assets rose, capital accumulation by Gulf states increased. Consequently, capital flows from these states to Amman resumed and construction activity started to pick up in the city.

Research problem and questions

The purpose of this book is to understand the influences of Gulf capital flows to Amman on the city's urban built environment and its megaprojects during the early twenty-first century. By Gulf capital flows, I mainly refer to the flow of state and private capital from the Arab Gulf states for the purpose of investment. The term Gulf capital as I use it here includes capital that originated in the Gulf, even that owned by non-Gulf nationals. It also includes capital originating in the Gulf that penetrates other national or international capital in the form of firm ownership ties and conglomerates. By the influences of capital flows on the urban built environment, I mean the impact of foreign investment in the production and consumption of the city's urban built environment: how this investment transforms the shape of the built environment in the city and produces it as a commodity. Megaprojects are defined here as major mixed-use large-scale developments costing between a few hundred million and several billion US dollars and having major impact on the city's urban fabric, as well as local communities and city residents.

The overarching question of this research is: how did Gulf capital flows to Amman influence the construction, production, and consumption of the city's megaprojects and its built environment and affect the city residents' identity in the early twenty-first century? Two interrelated sets of subquestions can help answer this central question.

First, how did Gulf capital flows to Amman in the early twenty-first century influence the city image, that is, the shape of the city's built environment and the city residents', and others', perception and understanding of this environment as well as the mental construction of the city?[4] How did Amman's recent megaprojects relate to the question of homogeneity, heterogeneity, and hybridity of the urban built environment under contemporary globalization's flows? How did the new megaprojects in the city, as well as the resulting transformation of Amman's urban built environment, and the city residents' interaction with these developments, fit into the capitalist economy and its modes of production?

Second, how did Amman's early twenty-first-century megaprojects and the city image produced and constructed through capital flows relate to the question of the city residents' identity? What identity or identities did these megaprojects and the discourses that accompanied them express or construct? How did the new megaprojects in Amman and the image of the city they created represent or create this identity? How did the developers' discourses, particularly advertisement, on these projects communicate the city residents' identity?

The scope of the book

Although this book addresses the relation between the processes of globalization and the urban built environment in Amman, it focuses on the influence of capital flows – specifically Gulf capital flows. The book addresses other flows of globalization only as they relate to the flow of capital and expand the arguments in this study. This is because I find capital flows the most significant flows of globalization for the transformation of the urban built environment in Amman in the early twenty-first century.

This book takes recent megaprojects in Amman as the study cases. Although transformations in Amman's urban built environment were not limited to the increasing production of megaprojects, capital flows to the city during the early twenty-first century were invested extensively in large-scale developments. The impact of such developments on the transformation of the urban built environment of Amman and the image of the city during the early twenty-first century was stronger than that of small-scale developments. Such large-scale developments are responsible for establishing new architectural vocabulary and building scale, changing the city's skyline and landscape. Moreover, megaprojects have a significant influence on changing the relation between Amman's residents and the urban built environment. Large-scale developments increasingly change the way people interact with their built environment and people's consumption patterns, and they help construct new collective identities. Furthermore, the discourses, particularly advertising discourse, which the developers created on the new megaprojects in Amman played an important role in creating the image of the city and shaping the identity of its residents. The fact that the state was a major player in several large-scale developments in the city, partly through public-private partnerships, adds to the significance of these developments for image and identity construction.

The time period selected for this study is the early twenty-first century because this is a period in which the urban built environment of Amman witnessed dramatic transformations inseparable from capital flows and global and regional integration of Jordan's economy. This was also a significant period in Jordan's history because after forty-six years of the former king's rule, there was a new head of state. Under the new king, King Abdullah II (r. 1999–present), Jordan's economic integration was strongly reinforced.

King Abdullah II has given high priority to improving Jordan's economy since he acceded to the throne (Henry & Springborg, 2010; Schlumberger, 2002), focusing "almost exclusively on economic reform during the first years of his reign" (Henry & Springborg, 2010, p. 253). Jordan's economic reform began in the 1990s. During this period, the country adopted policies of privatization, deregulation, and liberalization of the flow of capital and goods. The economic reform aimed at enhancing the country's competitiveness through the integration of Jordan's economy into the global economy, opening up the economy to international businesses and new markets (Schlumberger, 2002). Economic reform in Jordan moved rapidly in the early 2000s at a pace much faster than the reform in other Arab countries (Schlumberger, 2002). The reforms that took place during this period included expansion of privatization, new tax legislation, reform of landlord-tenant legislation,[5] vigorous marketing of Jordan's Qualifying Industrial Zones to potential investors (Henry & Springborg, 2010), development of private-public partnerships, and lifting fuel subsidies (OBG, 2009). The 2000s witnessed significant acceleration of the integration of Jordan's economy into the global economy (Henry & Springborg, 2010). The fast pace of the globalization of the country's economy is not surprising given Jordan's dependency on economic grants and international loans, which makes it important to "stay in the good graces of the international financial community" (p. 251). In 2000, Jordan joined the World Trade Organization (Henry & Springborg, 2010). The country also entered into a number of free trade agreements (FTAs) with several countries during the 2000s, which increased Jordan's exports considerably. These include an FTA with the United States in 2001, Singapore in 2005, and Canada in 2010 (OBG, 2008, 2009, 2010).

During the first decade of the twenty-first century, economic links between Jordan and the Arab Gulf states were renewed and strengthened. These had weakened in the early 1990s due to Jordan's stance on the 1990–1991 Gulf War and remained weak throughout the 1990s.[6] Capital flowed from the Gulf to Jordan, particularly between 2003 and 2007 as the economies of Gulf states became stronger and more diversified (Pfeifer, 2010). Jordan had by then opened up its economy and encouraged foreign investment. The country welcomed Gulf capital flows, and "King Abdullah stressed the importance of tapping into the massive liquidity . . . available in the GCC [Gulf Cooperation Council] states" (OBG, 2008, p. 31). In fact, following Hanieh (2011), it can be argued that the "internationalization of Gulf capital" drove the opening up of economy and neoliberal reform processes in Jordan, as much as it supported these processes. In 2008, Gulf investments in Jordan were estimated at USD16 billion, which accounted for 10 percent of Jordan's gross domestic product ("Investment boom," 2008). Given this integration of Jordan's economy into the regional and global economy, it was influenced by the global economic crisis. The economy had slowed down by late 2008 and continued to slow down in the next two years (see OBG, 2009). Thus, the early twenty-first century was a period in which new capital poured into Amman, causing a construction boom that was followed by severe cuts as the economic crisis hit the city, which in turn caused a slump in construction. This slump, however, eased in the 2010s as capital began to flow back to the city. This rise and fall makes the early twenty-first century an exemplary period for the purpose of analyzing the influences of Gulf capital flows on the city's urban built environment.

The significance of the book

This book contributes to the understanding of the urban built environment of globalizing cities. It fits into the emergent body of scholarly studies on architecture and urbanity of Arab cities during the late twentieth and early twenty-first centuries, which address processes such as the flow of capital, people, and information operating at global, regional, and national levels and strongly influencing the urban built environment. Elsheshtawy's two edited volumes *The Evolving Arab City* (2008) and *Planning Middle Eastern Cities* (2004) belong to this body of work. So do publications dedicated to the study of oil-rich cities where record-breaking developments in terms of scale and cost are taking place, such as Kanna's *Dubai: The City as Corporation* (2011) and his edited volume *The Superlative City* (2008), and Elsheshtawy's *Dubai: Behind an Urban Spectacle* (2010). To these may be added scholarly studies on cities that are in the center of events because of their suffering from political instabilities and war conflicts, such as Khalaf's *Heart of Beirut* (2006), and megalopolises that have always been the topic of study in academic publications on Islamic and colonial cities, such as Singerman and Amar's edited volume *Cairo Cosmopolitan* (2006).

Amman has not received commensurate attention in recent studies on globalizing cities. This may be attributed to a number of factors. Among these is the small economy of Jordan:[7] many of Amman's urban developments are simply overshadowed by developments taking place in oil-rich Arab states. Despite the fact that Jordan during the 2000s received over 10 percent of the capital flows from the Gulf states to the Middle East and North Africa (Pfeifer, 2010) and that investors from these states find Amman a good place for real estate investment, scholars have largely ignored the influence of such a condition on Amman's built environment. Another factor is the size of Amman. With a population of four million inhabitants (Department of Statistics [DOS], 2016), Amman is not a large city by world standards. The city's significant and sudden growth due to reasons beyond Jordan's geographic boundaries, such as the ongoing Syrian

Civil War and the 2003 Iraqi War and the subsequent fleeing of Syrians and Iraqis to Amman, and the diversity of the city's population are conditions that scholarly writings on Amman's built environment have not addressed adequately. A third factor that may account for Amman's near absence in recent studies on globalizing cities is that the city is not in the center of contentious political events. Jordan is politically stable, although it sits in a turbulent region with conflicts in the West Bank and Israel to the west, in Iraq to the east, and in Syria to the north, not to mention the unstable political situation in nearby Lebanon. Thus, there are no recent lengthy studies on the influences of globalization's flows on the urban built environment of early twenty-first-century Amman, nor studies on the influences of Gulf capital flows. Furthermore, there are no recent studies that address the relation between identity, discourse, capital flows, and the built environment in Amman. The research of this book, therefore, fills gaps in scholarly studies on the built environment of Amman, as well as the general built environment of globalizing Arab and Middle Eastern cities.

The significance of this study goes beyond filling gaps in scholarly work on architecture and urbanism. It shows how Amman, like any other Muslim or non-Muslim, Arab or non-Arab, or Middle Eastern or Western city, is shaped by diverse and ever-changing economic, political, and sociocultural forces. By investigating how economic forces, particularly Gulf capital flows, influenced the city in the early twenty-first century, this book moves beyond the study of Arab cities as a mere product of religion or colonization to understand the city as it evolved under the current condition of regional and global interconnectedness. Modern Amman has always been shaped by economic, political, and sociocultural forces outside its geographic boundaries, even outside the state's boundaries.[8] Amman's continuing attraction of capital from the Gulf states during most of the 2000s and the impact of the 2008 global economic crisis on the city make it an interesting case for the study of the influences of capital flows. Considering that during the early twenty-first century Amman's built environment underwent dramatic transformations at both the architectural and urban scales, which seen from the narrow perspective of local and national forces do not make much sense in light of economic conditions of the city's population,[9] the study of Amman's built environment as it relates to global economic processes becomes significant for understanding urban transformations in the city.

Theoretical framework

Theoretical conceptions

The theoretical framework of this book is based on the work of David Harvey on urban development and capitalism, Michel Foucault on power relations and discourse, and Benedict Anderson on identity. Together, these works allow for an analysis of the influences of capital flows on Amman's urban built environment at the macro-level of interstate, state, institutions, and class, on the one hand, and the micro-level of the individual who can exercise power understood in the Foucauldian sense and whose taste and identity are increasingly evolving and reconstructed through the interaction with various flows of globalization and through discursive formations.

Using the theories of Harvey and Foucault presents some challenges to this study, not least because they originate from a context different from this study. Foucault's theory comes from his study of knowledge, power, and ethics in a Western European context. In such a context, Foucault (1975/1995) finds disciplinary power to have partly replaced and partly worked along with sovereign power. Foucault refers to disciplinary power as a "technology" that consists of "a whole set of instruments, techniques, procedures, levels of application, [and] targets" (p. 215) and may be exercised by institutions, such as a prison, school, hospital, or family, or by a state apparatus such as the police. Unlike sovereign power, disciplinary power is "exercised," not simply "held." It is exercised "over" and "through" the individual and groups of individuals to regulate their behavior (Dean, 1999, p. 19). It is challenging, but not impossible, to use Foucault's notion of disciplinary power in a non-Western context such as Jordan, where sovereign power cannot be overestimated.[10]

Another challenge, albeit one more easily overcome, is that Harvey's theory focuses on what he refers to as "advanced capitalist" societies in the context of Western Europe and North America. Amman's, and Jordan's, economy does not follow the advanced capitalist system Harvey studies. Scholars such as Peter Hall and David Soskice speak of varieties of capitalism (Hall, 1998; McDonough, Reich, & Kotz, 2010). Different frameworks of political economy institutions in capitalist economies lead to "systematic differences in corporate strategies" in these economies (McDonough et al., 2010, p. 7). Henry and Springborg (2010) argue that capital-rich countries in the Middle East and North Africa were likely to adopt the Anglo-American model of capitalism, whereas capital-poor countries adopted the German model, which is better "adapted to situations of capital scarcity" and "offers protection to capital-scarce economies" (p. 15). Unlike the advanced Anglo-American capitalism, which is "shareholder-centered and impatient" (McDonough et al., 2010, p. 7) and characterized by highly competitive markets for the sale and exchange of stocks and bonds with a variety of actors (Henry & Springborg, 2010), the German model of capitalism is a "bank-centered and patient capitalism" (McDonough et al., 2010, p. 7), which emphasizes private-sector capitalist activities of universal banks – not individual investors – who can exercise power over the government to provide conditions attractive for businesses (Henry & Springborg,

2010). Jordan's economy follows the German capitalist model. In addition to formal legislative and institutional frameworks, informal sociopolitical patterns have a bearing on the form of economy in Jordan (Schlumberger, 2002). Social norms such as patronage, favoritism, loyalty to family, clan, and tribe, and rent-seeking are dominant in Jordan, permeating political and economic activity and holding Jordan back from embracing advanced capitalism (Schlumberger, 2002).[11]

The use of Anderson's (2006) theorization of imagined communities and constructed identity in the context of Amman is less of a challenge than the use of Foucault's and Harvey's theory. For despite the significance of the European and American contexts for Anderson's theorization, Anderson extends his theorization to include colonial effects on the construction of the identity of colonized societies and postcolonial nation-states, a context with which Jordan, particularly Amman, can very much identify. The British created the Jordanian state under the British Mandate and chose Amman as its capital. Furthermore, they established colonial institutions, such as the military, that were influential in constructing the Jordanian identity.

Another challenge in using the theories of Harvey, Foucault, and, to a lesser degree, Anderson is that they all engage space at different scales and levels of detail than I do in this study. This is in part because they come from outside the discipline of architecture: Harvey is a geographer, Foucault is a philosopher and psychologist, and Anderson is a political scientist. This is also partly because they use the scale of space that serves their projects and arguments best and demonstrates their perspectives. Thus, Harvey often studies space at a large scale: the scale of whole cities and the globe at large. He also addresses space at a relatively small scale such as in his treatment of megaprojects in Baltimore, USA, and the Canary Wharf development, UK. Foucault engages the small scale of the individual building in his theorization. So he studies the prison, the asylum, and the clinic as institutions as well as spatial organizations inseparable from the logic behind their "birth," to borrow Foucault's word. Again, this is no surprise given the emphasis of Foucault's project on the microscale of power. Anderson engages the scale of the state, which serves his purpose of understanding identity as it relates to the nation-state, and touches upon the scale of the individual building.

Combining the theories of Harvey, Foucault, and Anderson, which is uncommon in scholarly works, presents another challenge I undertake in this study. This is particularly the case in combining Harvey's and Foucault's theories, which at first seem to be irreconcilable, not least because of their emphasis on different levels and natures of power. Foucault's power is the micro-power of the individual exercised in different social activities. Harvey's power is the macro-power of capital, the capitalist class, and the capitalist state with its political-economy system. Harvey is often criticized for not engaging Foucault's work, as well as other postmodernist theory, in his theorization of urban space and capitalism. According to Katz (2006), Harvey's failure to engage theory that addresses different power relations at different scales left his project economically deterministic and totalizing. Such a critique is only partly valid.

A close reading of Harvey's work shows that he acknowledges forces other than the capitalist economy in the production of the urban built environment, although non-economic forces remain underplayed and secondary to the economic force in his theorization of the urban built environment. Harvey (1989, 1990) pays attention to detail within his meta-theory of capital and recognizes differences even inside the capitalist class. Furthermore, he points out the significance of

> the treatment of difference and 'otherness' not as something to be added on to more fundamental Marxist categories . . . but as something that should be omni-present from the very beginning in any attempt to grasp the dialectics of social change.
>
> (1990, p. 355)

Harvey also speaks of power at the microscale of the individual or a group of individuals and does not rule out the possibility that those who are subject to the macro-power of the capitalist state and capitalist class would resist that power. Thus, although Harvey adopts the idea that power is a system of domination, he admits that such domination does not necessarily always succeed.

Harvey (1990) convincingly argues that, under the current condition in which global capital has command over space, the concern for differences and otherness and the emphasis on the micro-power of the individual should not lead to the denial of the macro-power of capital or its dismissal as irrelevant. Harvey criticizes postmodernists, including Foucault, for avoiding the discussion of the power of money in what he calls "money economies," particularly in capitalist societies. For him, the power of money in capitalist societies is a pressing issue. Harvey, therefore, argues that postmodernists should not avoid the power of capital and its institutions, including the capitalist state, in their work on the urban built environment. Despite Foucault's downplaying of macro-powers such as that of the capitalist state, he acknowledges that the macro-power of the capitalist state does exist. According to Foucault (1980), he did not mean to undermine the effectiveness of the state's power; neither did he want to put excessive emphasis on the state, because this would risk portraying it as having an exclusive power and thus undermine other mechanisms of power, which do not necessarily operate through state apparatuses. In other words, Foucault (1984/2003,

p. 35) does not rule out the idea that there exists "states of domination" within power relations. He acknowledges the power of the state, although he stresses that it does not play an exclusive role (Foucault, 1980). Foucault (1984/2003, p. 35) disagrees that "power is a system of domination that controls everything and leaves no room for freedom."

Whereas Harvey's project focuses on the macroscale of power and deemphasizes power at the microscale, Foucault's project focuses on the microscale of power and deemphasizes power at the macroscale. And while Harvey emphasizes the power of money economy, particularly the capitalist economy, over other powers, Foucault emphasizes the dispersal of power in all social activities and plays down the power of money economy. Taken alone, neither of these two approaches is adequate for understanding transformations in the urban built environment under the condition of contemporary globalization. Bringing together Harvey's and Foucault's understanding of power relations – the macro-power and micro-power, the power of a money economy as well as other powers – can help better understand contemporary architectural and urban production in Amman.

Theoretical conceptions as used in this book

Harvey's theorization of urban development as integral to the capitalist mode of production is helpful in understanding the role of capital flows in the transformation of Amman's urban built environment and how this transformation fits into capitalist production processes. Following Harvey, I begin from the assumption that the power of money economy is predominant in producing the urban built environment and investigate the degree to which capitalists' power and values drove Amman's megaprojects in the early twenty-first century. I particularly study how capital flows to the city intensified creative destruction, introducing new forms of social relations in the city. I investigate what the process of creative destruction involved in the context of Amman where industrial production – an important aspect in Harvey's (1989, 1990, 2005) conception of creative destruction as it relates to urban development – was small. I also study transformations of the city's urban built environment as they relate to the construction of the city image, understood as the shape of the built environment and the ways it is perceived by the city residents as well as the mental construction of this environment, and the relation of the new city image to the capitalist economy. In addition, I study the commodification of Amman's urban built environment in the early twenty-first century and its relation to capitalists' logic of profit-making and continuous growth. I also investigate how the city's contemporary image and commodified spaces were a means to construct

Amman as a global city and, thus, increase the city's and the country's integration into the global economy.

Despite the significance of Harvey's theorization for understanding the urban built environment, particularly for a study such as this that deals with the influences of the flow of capital on transforming the built environment, it remains inadequate for attaining a comprehensive understanding. The power of money, understood in relation to capitalist modes of production, is not the only power at play when it comes to shaping the urban built environment. Sociocultural and ideological forces as well as political forces, other than the political-economy force that Harvey emphasizes, have a strong bearing on the production of the urban built environment. Those forces involve power relations of different natures and at different scales. Harvey himself acknowledges forces other than economy and discusses differences among capitalists and the play of power at a microscale among them, although he remains focused on the macro-power of the capitalist economy. Thus, even a study that focuses on the economic force and recognizes the significance of a macro-power, such as that of corporate capitalists for shaping the urban built environment in ways that produce value and stimulate consumption, should not dismiss the agency of other groups and individuals as irrelevant. Agency is the capacity of the actor, whether an individual or a group of people, to exert power or "some degree of control over the social relations in which . . . [the actor] is enmeshed, which in turn implies the ability to transform those social relations to some degree" (Sewel, 1992, p. 20). Emphasis on capitalists' agency in the production of the urban built environment reveals a significant part of the backdrop against which the urban built environment in Amman is produced. But, this emphasis does not help identify other agencies, which, for example, may help us understand the reason behind the use of different architectural vocabularies in Amman's new developments. True, Harvey (2001) argues that under global capital flows, marks of distinction are important for the command of the market. But, his theorization does not help us understand why marks of distinction translate into this or that architectural vocabulary in the urban built environment in the same context. By itself, Harvey's approach to the urban built environment does not explain the different ideologies and the subjectivity of decision-makers, such as national or foreign planners and architects, and local legislators, who contribute to the production of the built environment. Moreover, Harvey's theorization falls short when it comes to understanding how different city residents exercise power as they interact with and make sense of their built environment in multiple ways.

Thus, Harvey's approach to understanding the urban built environment needs to be complemented by a bottom-up, microscale approach. Here the work of Foucault is helpful. Using Foucault's notion of micro-power helps us understand how individuals in Amman, be they city officials, architects, or users from different segments of society, exercised power at different levels and forms as they interacted with their built environment, playing an active role in determining the shape, use, and meaning of developments in the city and contributing to the success or failure of capitalists' agenda behind the production of the urban built environment. Combining Foucault's and Harvey's theorizations makes it possible to understand what agencies were involved in the production and consumption of the built environment in Amman and how such agencies intersected. Using Harvey's and Foucault's theorizations, we can start to talk about the agency of corporate capitalists as producers of Amman's megaprojects, the agency of high state and city officials as decision-makers and legislators, the agency of architects as authors of the design, and the agency of the city residents as users and consumers of the urban built environment.

I also use Harvey's and Foucault's theories of power relations, along with Anderson's notion of identity constructedness, to understand how recent transformations of the urban built environment in Amman with the power relations embedded in them communicated, and contributed to the construction of, the city residents' identity. Following Anderson (2006), I take identity, including national identity, as a construct, not as an essential thing that has always been there and will always be the same. Based on this conception, and as Massad (2001) argues, people's identity in Amman, including their national identity, is constructed. As such, this identity and the ways it is negotiated in the city's built environment are constantly evolving, continuously shaped and reshaped with the changing economic, political, and sociocultural circumstances in the city, which are inseparable from global and regional forces. Thus, I study how Amman's early twenty-first-century megaprojects played a role in representing the city residents' identity, or identities, and investigate different agencies involved in the construction of this identity through the city's urban built environment and its expression in this environment. These agencies include a macro-power such as that of the capitalist economy, which is inseparable from the power of the state and creates and promotes certain identity, or identities, that will serve the interest of those who hold this power. Another significant agency in identity negotiation through the city's built environment is the agency of individuals or groups of individuals such as architects, planners, and city residents, who may exercise power at the microscale, contributing to identity construction and expressing certain identities in the built environment.

I use Foucault's (1969/1972) notion of discourse as constructive of meanings and reality, or the objects of which it speaks, to investigate the role of discourse, including advertisement, that accompanied contemporary megaprojects in constructing Amman as a global city. I analyze advertising discourse to understand how this discourse, through the images and texts it transmits, creates the image of the city, defines certain norms regarding what a perfect lifestyle is, and conveys the city residents' identity. I also use Foucault's (1975/1995, 1976/2003, 1974/2007) and Harvey's (1989, 1990, 1991) understanding of discourse as produced through power relations to investigate how power, be it at the macroscale or microscale, played in the production of advertising discourse on Amman's urban built environment as well as in the interpretation of this discourse. Using Harvey's theory of the macro-power of capitalists, I investigate how the developers' discourses promote certain ideas – those of the capitalists – over others to support the interests of capitalist businesses and the capitalist class. In this light, I regard the discourses, particularly advertising discourse, that accompanied Amman's contemporary megaprojects as intended to persuade the consumers or audience of this discourse that they needed to consume, that is, buy, lease, or frequently use, the advertised developments, which after all were integral to capitalist modes of production. Their consumption was necessary to produce the growth of capitalists' capital. Capitalists convince audiences to consume their products, constructing the audiences' identities in a fashion that ultimately will serve capitalists' interests. Using Foucault's theory of the micro-power of the individual, I investigate how the audience read or interpreted the developers' discourses and whether they exercised power to resist the producers' preferred reading of advertisements and other discourse by the developers, thus resisting the corporate power. The audience might understand advertising discourse in ways different from what the producers of this discourse intended, and different individuals might make different sense of this discourse. This discourse might overwhelm the audience and place some restriction on their power to resist, particularly when seen as a part of media discourse that promoted similar ideas serving the interest of big businesses.

Research methods

The study in this book relies on qualitative research. It is a multiple-case study in which I investigate the research problem through the analysis of three bounded cases of megaprojects in Amman. The research combines several methods. I reviewed relevant theoretical literary work and recent textual as well as visual resources on early twenty-first-century Amman, including resources on the city's economy and global economic integration, its residents' culture and identity, recent physical transformations in the city, and the study cases. This material includes scholarly writings, local newspaper articles, statistical records, municipal documents, maps and aerial views of the sites of the case study developments, real estate supplements and magazines, and promotional and marketing material as well as architectural and urban designs of the study cases. In addition, I made multiple visits between 2008 and 2015 to the megaproject cases analyzed in this book, photographing them and recording observations of them and their context.

In 2010 I conducted face-to-face interviews with stakeholders: those involved in, influenced by, or having a concern or interest in the city's megaprojects, including decision-makers, professionals, and city residents. I designed the interviews in a semi-structured manner where some questions and the order in which they were presented were predetermined, but the questions were open-ended. This allowed me to adjust the questions to the immediate situation, thus increasing rapport, and to pursue unanticipated topics. For the interviews with decision-makers and professionals, I selected the sample of interviewees for their prominent roles in the selected developments or for their wide knowledge about the city's urban built environment and its recent transformation. Among the interviewees were city officials at Greater Amman Municipality (GAM), executive officers at investment and development corporations, and architects as well as planners who designed projects included in the study cases. I also interviewed other prominent architects who, although they did not design any of the projects included in this study, are considered influential figures in shaping Amman's urban built environment directly, through their designs, and indirectly, through their influence on the works of a younger generation of architects practicing in the city. In addition, I interviewed planning and architecture academics who were involved in some of the study cases or who influence the direction of the city's architecture through their research work and critical writing.

I interviewed ordinary citizens to understand the ways people made sense of and assigned meanings to transformations in Amman's megaprojects in the early twenty-first century, how they interpreted the developers' discourse on recent developments in the city, how this discourse affected people's perception of their built environment, and how contemporary urban developments in Amman and the discourse accompanying them related to the question of people's identity and its negotiation in the built environment. I used purposeful sampling (also known as nonprobability sampling) to select the sample of interviewees. Purposeful sampling involves the selection of interviewees because "they can purposefully inform an understanding of the research problem and central phenomenon in the study" (Creswell, 2007, p. 125). Following Creswell's maximum variation sampling strategy, I selected the interviewees based on six criteria: physical distance from the site of the study case; age group; education level; exposure to non-Jordanian culture through living abroad for an extended period; social class; and place of origin, as Amman has a complex demographic structure, which is particularly relevant when it comes to understanding identity as it relates to recent transformations in the city's built environment. Together, these criteria provide many possible combinations of criteria, allowing for maximum diversification of interviewees. The diverse research participants shared a wide spectrum of views regarding Amman's recent megaprojects, which enriched the research discussion and findings.

I conducted cross-case analysis of the extensive and detailed data collected from the multiple information sources. This thematic analysis ran across the cases to illustrate the issue under study from different perspectives. I looked for similarities and differences among cases and the possibilities for developing generalizations concerning the influences of Gulf capital flows on Amman's urban built environment and its residents' identity in the early twenty-first century. I used the categories I formed from my reading of the interview responses, field notes, and the developers' discourse, as well as the categories implicated in my research subquestions and drawn from the literature review to identify and develop the study's themes and subthemes and organize the narrative of this book thematically.

Overview of the urban built environment of Amman in the early twenty-first century

It was not uncommon for visitors to Amman in the twentieth century to call the city a "sleepy" or "provincial" city (United Nations, 2005, p. 7). "This is a nice small town," said a visitor to Amman in the late 1990s.[12] Similarly, non-Jordanians I interviewed during my fieldwork research who lived in Amman in the late 1990s described the city back then as sleepy. But, early twenty-first-century Amman was neither small nor sleepy. The real estate and construction sectors in the city witnessed significant growth during the 2000s (OBG, 2009). This growth, and the attractive market of the booming Gulf states, resulted in a shortage of skilled labor in the construction sector in 2007 (OBG, 2008) and shortage of experienced architects and engineers in Amman.[13] By the end of the 2000s, Amman's urban area had expanded from around 130 square kilometers in the early 1990s to 280 square kilometers.[14]

The economic conditions of the 2000s encouraged investment in Jordan, including investment in the urban built environment. During this period, the demand for houses and other services in Amman increased, contributing to rising property prices. The 2003 Iraqi War and the continued political and economic instability in Iraq contributed significantly to this situation. The affluent segment of Iraqis in Amman increased demand for high-end residential and commercial developments. Furthermore, Jordan emerged as a "major gateway for business with Iraq" (OBG, 2009, p. 29) and a base for government and non-government organizations operating in Iraq (OBG, 2008). These conditions, along with Jordan's strategic geographic location and its image as a peaceful country amid a troubled region, made Jordan, particularly Amman, attractive to real estate investors. Between 2001 and 2008, one hundred non-Jordanian construction firms, most of which were based in the Gulf, were registered in Jordan ("Investment boom," 2008). Investors from the Arab Gulf states hoped to "reproduce the lucrative Dubai real estate model, albeit in a far more modest scale, in Jordan" (OBG, 2009, p. 29).

Planning policies in Amman encouraged real estate investment in the city. Following a call from King Abdullah II to create a comprehensive plan for Amman, Greater Amman Municipality, in collaboration with local and Western experts, embarked on a master plan for the city in 2006, called the Amman Plan (Greater Amman Municipality [GAM], 2008). This plan aimed, among other things, to develop Amman into an efficient, green, sustainable city that would become a destination for investors and tourists. The Amman Plan, which took into consideration Amman's projected population in 2025 (six million people) consisted of plans at three scales: the metropolitan scale, which addressed the growth strategy for Greater Amman; the area scale, which included land use and major road network plans for the eight areas of Greater Amman; the community scale, which included detailed plans for neighborhoods and blocks (GAM, 2008). The plans at the community scale included regulations for the location of high-rise buildings in the city and design guidelines for these buildings (GAM, 2008; also see GAM, 2007a). These plans also included a strategy for corridor intensification: the identification of urban transport corridors and the introduction of policies, plans, and guidelines for the development of vacant land in existing urban areas along these corridors (GAM, 2007b, 2008). The Amman Plan created a "one-stop shop" that would facilitate application and review processes for large-scale projects (GAM, 2007a, 2007b). Instead of submitting their designs for different authorities, investors would submit these designs only to GAM, which would follow up on these submissions with relevant authorities (GAM, 2007a, 2007b).

Influenced by the local, regional, and global forces mentioned earlier, Amman underwent an unprecedented construction boom, which changed the shape of the city dramatically. Parker (2009) describes early twenty-first-century Amman well in the following passage:

> Jordan's capital appears as a city of holes. In between detours necessitated by work at strategic points along the city's road network, one encounters numerous fenced off construction zones spruced up with

billboards that provide a glimpse of the glittering future in store for the site.

(p. 110)

The new Amman, as Parker pointed out, was to conform to "globalized benchmarks of speed, efficiency, and connectivity" (2009, p. 110). To obtain the speed and connectivity necessary to encourage globalization's flows, particularly capital flows, the availability of efficient transport and communication networks in the city was essential. Thus, Amman underwent increasing developments in this vein since the early 2000s. Many underpasses and overpasses were constructed in Amman during this period. The Abdoun Bridge in Western Amman is among the latest and most monumental overpasses in the city. Completed in 2006 and designed by Dar al-Handasah (Shair and Partners), this bridge became an icon of Amman, appearing on the city's promotional material and national TV. The city also upgraded the Amman Queen Alia International Airport to serve nine million passengers per year, which is more than triple the number of passengers the airport previously served, and the designs permit future expansion to serve twelve million passengers per year. The internationally renowned British firm Foster and Partners was the main architect for the new airport, which opened in 2013 (see "Queen Alia International Airport," n.d.).

The influence of money flows to the city, as architect Ayman Zuaiter pointed out, could literally be identified in Amman's early twenty-first-century built environment where multiple branches of banks, occupying carefully designed buildings, dotted the city's landscape (personal communication, September 2, 2010). A review of building licenses issued by the Jordan Engineers Association (JEA) in the past two decades reveals that the number of bank buildings licensed in Amman was remarkably high in the 2000s compared to that in the 1990s. This is understandable considering that in the 2000s around 90 percent of the national banks in Jordan included significant Gulf investment (Hanieh, 2011). The review of JEA's building licenses shows that the number of other commercial buildings licensed in the 2000s also was much higher than those licensed in the 1990s. In addition, JEA's licenses reveal a jump in the number of building licenses and the total licensed area in 2004, which can be seen as an influence of Gulf investment as well as the 2003 Iraqi War. Although construction statistics in Amman show that the private sector's contribution to building construction in the city during the 2000s was much more than that of the public sector (DOS, 2007), many developments categorized as private-sector-owned, in reality were undertaken under a public-private partnership. This is no wonder given that public-private partnership approach to business in Amman, and Jordan at large, was among the important economic reforms the state adopted in the 2000s to encourage economic global integration and enhance the country's economy.

As some in the city commented, the fast pace of construction activities in the first decade of the twenty-first century negatively influenced the special character of Amman's built environment (R. Badran & A. Zuaiter, personal communications, September 1–2, 2010; Malkawi & Kaddoura, 2007). The urban fabric no longer reflected the city's topography, and the distinctive undulating nature of Amman's skyline was interrupted (see Figure 1.1). Furthermore, the built environment in Amman lacked harmony as buildings of different scales, materials, shapes, and architectural vocabularies were haphazardly scattered around the city (see Malkawi & Kaddoura, 2007). The use of stone on buildings had helped hide some of the chaos in Amman's built environment, as Swiss architect Mario Botta once commented.[15] But as observation of recent developments in the city reveals and as architects in Amman agree, glass and other sheathing and finishing materials new to the city were increasingly used on buildings. Even when stone was used as a finishing material, the large scale of the developments made the disparity between individual developments and their context hard to dismiss.

Figure 1.1 View of the skyline of Amman from the Dabouq area in Western Amman. The remarkably tall two buildings of the Jordan Gate development appear in the background in the center left.

Note: Taken by the author on January 23, 2010.

Introduction to the study cases

For this study, three megaprojects were analyzed: The New Downtown, Jordan Gate, and Sanaya Amman. These are representative of large-scale urban developments that took place, or were planned to take place, in Amman in the early twenty-first century. It is, therefore, appropriate to use these developments as a lens through which a globalizing Amman can be understood and answers to the research questions posed earlier can be sought.

The New Downtown of Amman (Abdali)

This project is locally known as *Mashru' al-'Abdali*, Arabic for the Abdali project, and often abbreviated as Abdali (Figure 1.2). Abdali is also the name of the area where the project is located, a central area in Amman (Figure 1.3). As documents by the developers show, the Abdali project is a public-private partnership (Abdali Investment and Development [AID], 2010, 2015). The state's share in this development is about 44 percent of the project's shares (Reuters, 2010), which consists of the state-owned land the project occupies. The New Downtown is undertaken by Abdali Investment and Development (AID), a privately owned land development firm consisting of a joint venture of three firms (AID, 2010, 2015). The first is the financially and administratively independent state-owned real estate developer National Resources Investment & Development Corporation (Mawared), which is owned by the Jordanian military and was founded to "oversee the transfer of military sites to private developers" (Parker, 2009, p. 115). The second is the privately owned Horizon Group, an international real estate investment and development conglomerate (AID, 2010, 2015), the original capital of which was made in the Gulf by the Saudi-naturalized Lebanese Hariri family.[16] The third is the privately owned United Real Estate Company–Jordan, a part of the group Kuwait Projects Company (KIPCO; AID, 2010, 2015). Together, the two non-Jordanian firms Horizon and United Real Estate hold about 56 percent of the Abdali project's shares (Reuters, 2010). The Beirut-based LACECO Architects & Engineers prepared the master plan and design guidelines for this development (AID, 2010; R. Abou Rayan & G. Amireh, personal communications, August 2 and 8, 2010). In addition to AID and national investment firms, a number of international investors, mainly based in the Gulf, have acquired land plots for development within the project's area. According to a list of investors involved in Phase I of the Abdali development, which was prepared in 2008 and procured from AID in 2010, around 60 percent of the built-up area would be developed by non-Jordanian developers, primarily from UAE and Kuwait. The remaining 40 percent of the built-up area would be developed by Jordanian developers. The list showed that Gulf capital penetration into

Figure 1.2 View of the Abdali development looking west toward the high-rise building of Rotana Hotel.

Note: Taken by May Musa on July 15, 2016.

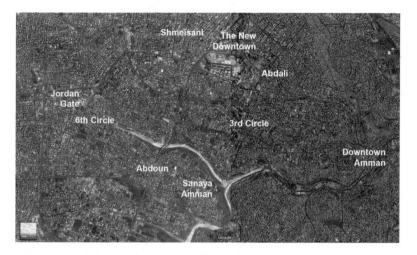

Figure 1.3 Map of Amman showing the sites of the study cases and their surroundings.

large-scale projects in the Abdali development was more than its penetration into relatively small-scale projects. A review of a recent Abdali developers' brochure shows that Gulf capital continues to play a similar role in this development, although this capital is not necessarily owned by the same corporations mentioned in AID's previous documents (see AID, 2015). For example, large-scale projects such as Rotana Hotel and The Lofts and The Heights are developed by the Abu-Dhabi-based Tourism Investment Company and the Dubai-based DAMAC respectively, and other major projects are being developed by or in joint venture with AID.

Work on the plans for the Abdali development began in 2001–2002 (F. Rabi, M. Rihani, & Y. Rajjal, personal communications, January, August, and September 2010). Construction work on the project began in 2004 (H. Abu Hijleh, personal communication, August 2, 2010). The project originally was scheduled to be completed in three phases (OBG, 2009). Phase I was scheduled to be completed in 2010 (AID, 2008; OBG, 2009), but was delayed as a result of the 2008 economic crisis. By 2014 many developments in this phase had become open to the public. Other developments were completed in the next two years, but a number of projects in Phase I of Abdali are yet to be completed. Work on Phase II is still in the very early stages. AID is silent about Phase III, which seems to have been put on hold as recent AID documents on the Abdali development speak of two phases of this project, not three. The New Downtown will occupy an area of over 380 *dunums*,[17] and it has an estimated cost of USD5 billion (AID, 2015). Phases I and II of this development will have a built-up area of two million square meters (AID, n.d., 2015).

Among the most important buildings in the Abdali neighborhood are those located east of the project's site (Figure 1.4). Next to the Abdali development is the Court of Law building. The headquarters for the Housing Bank for Trade and Finance is located east of the Court, and north of this bank is the Parliament building. Across the street and east of the bank are King Abdullah I Mosque (Figure 1.5) and the Ministry of Education. A church is located across the street south of the mosque and ministry. A few hundred meters east of the Abdali development used to be the busy Abdali transport hub, which has recently been relocated. Some three kilometers east of the Abdali development is the downtown of Amman. To the south of the Abdali development and across the street are modest low-rise commercial and residential buildings, military buildings, and Mawared's headquarters. Next to the Abdali development on the north are low-rise residential buildings. The northern and western borders of this development face the relatively affluent Shmeisani district, the financial and administrative district of Amman where many banks, government and financial institutions, and hotels are located. The western end of the Abdali development occupies the site of the Central Intelligence Agency (locally known as *al-Mukhabarat*), which was relocated to the outskirts of the city.

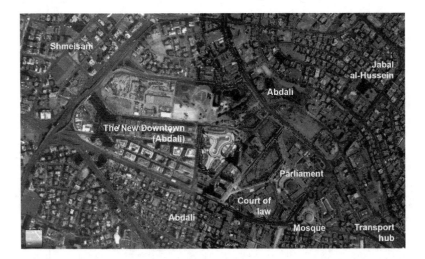

Figure 1.4 Map of The New Downtown site and its surroundings.

Figure 1.5 View of King Abdullah I Mosque across the street east of the Abdali development.

Note: Taken by the author on February 13, 2010.

Jordan Gate

The name Jordan Gate is a translation of the Arabic name Bawwabat al-Urdun. When the development was conceived in the early 2000s, I recall listening to comments in professional circles on the logic behind this development's name. The project, it was mentioned, will serve as the visitor's gateway to the Jordanian political and economic capital, thus to Jordan, as the visitor approaches Western Amman from the airport. Jordan Gate is located in the affluent area of the Sixth Circle in Western Amman, some thirty-five kilometers from the airport (see Figures 1.3 and 1.6). The developers of this project are the Bahrain-based Gulf Finance House, the Kuwait-based Kuwait Finance and Investment, the Kuwait-based Bayan Holding Company, and the UAE-based Al Hamad Contracting Company (Hazaimeh, 2007, 2010; "Wad' hajar," 2005).[18] The architects for this development are the Amman-based Consolidated Consultants-Jafar Tukan Architects (J. Tukan, personal communication, July 18, 2010). The project was begun in 2005 (Hazaimeh,

Figure 1.6 View of Jordan Gate and its surroundings from the Sixth Circle. In the
foreground on the right is the Crowne Plaza hotel.

Note: Taken by the author on January 23, 2010.

2007; "Wad' hajar," 2005), and it was scheduled to be completed by the end
of 2008 ("Injaz 80%," 2008). The developers rescheduled the completion of
this development more than once, with 2018 as the new expected completion
year ("GFH's Jordan Gate," 2010; Hazaimeh, 2010; Namrouqa, 2016).

Figure 1.7 View of Jordan Gate and its surroundings looking south. In the foreground on the left and right are residential buildings. In the background
are the Crowne Plaza hotel and the water tower in the center, and Jordan
Gate on the right.

Note: Taken by the author on January 23, 2010.

The USD300 million Jordan Gate occupies a site of 28.5 *dunums* and has
a built-up area of 220,000 square meters (Gulf Finance House B.S.C., 2006–
2007; Hazaimeh, 2007, 2010; "Wad' hajar," 2005). The project is located
on three relatively narrow streets, which border it on the north, south, and
west. The interviews I conducted with relevant individuals showed that
plans were made to widen one of these streets, to the extent the surrounding
urban fabric allowed, but the additional width of the street would serve as
a parking lane for vehicles of visitors to Jordan Gate. Located next to this
development on the east is the five-star Crowne Plaza Amman hotel (also
known locally by its previous name 'Amra Hotel; Figure 1.6). The three-
star San Rock Hotel is located across the street north of Jordan Gate, and
a water tower stands near the northeastern corner of this development. The
rest of the area surrounding Jordan Gate basically includes single-family
houses, villas, and low-rise residential buildings with small commercial
businesses at their bases, such as a bookstore, a studio, a dry cleaner, and a
grocery (see Figure 1.7).

Sanaya Amman (Limitless Towers)

According to the developers of this project, the name Sanaya, which they said is Arabic for "starlight" ("Green, innovative," 2009), was chosen because the project is "designed to make optimum use of . . . natural light by day, while illuminating the skyline of Amman at night" (p. 28). The Sanaya project (Figure 1.8) is best known in Amman for its earlier name, Limitless Towers, after its developers the Dubai-based real estate development company Limitless, a subsidiary of Dubai World (see Damra, 2009). The Chicago-based Murphy/Jahn served as the architects and main consultants for this project (Dwairi, 2008), and the Consolidated Consultants-Jafar Tukan Architects were the local coordinators and supervising engineers. The USD300 million development has a total built-up area of 173,000 square meters (Hazaimeh, 2008; "UAE firm," 2008).

Construction was begun on the Sanaya development in July 2008. The project was scheduled to be completed in 2011 (Damra, 2009; Dwairi, 2008), but the troubled financial situation of Dubai World and Limitless resulted in delays in construction work, putting the project on hold by the end of 2009 (see Reuters, 2009; Walter, 2010). Indeed work on the development has not moved beyond excavation. When I visited the site in 2010, it consisted of a construction fence around the site, project construction signs, and a foundation hole some 124 meters long, 74 meters wide, and 40 meters deep.[19] A recent Google aerial view of the area shows an empty site and a damaged landscape.

The site of Sanaya is located in Wadi Abdoun on a vacant lot previously owned by GAM (Figure 1.3). In the vicinity of the Sanaya site on the Abdoun side are middle-class low-rise residential buildings, single-family houses, and many vacant plots. Sparse low- and mid-rise buildings are located along the western road to the Sanaya site on the Jabal Amman side. Across the streets from this development, which is located at one of the corners of a major intersection in the older section of Amman, are modest low-rise residential and commercial buildings. According to a city official, the state had bought land in the area, particularly in the Qeisiyyah working-class neighborhood, for the development of a government district that will include many government institution buildings (M. Awamleh, personal communication, September 5, 2010), but this development has yet to materialize.

The structure of the book

This chapter has stated the research problem and questions. It has defined the scope of the book, its significance, and its place in recent scholarly publications on globalizing cities, particularly Arab and Middle Eastern cities. The chapter has set the theoretical framework of the book and described the research methods. In addition, it has presented a background of the urban

Figure 1.8 3D view of the Sanaya Amman development.

Note: Adapted by Nora Eltayeib from Limitless's promotional material of Sanaya Amman.

built environment in early twenty-first-century Amman and introduced the megaprojects that constitute the study cases of this book.

Chapter 2, Constructing Global Amman, provides thematic analysis of the study cases to show how contemporary megaprojects in Amman, which were produced mainly through the investment of Gulf capital in the city, and the developers' discourse on these projects create the city as a global city. This chapter consists of three main sections. The first, Creative Destruction, argues that the production of recent megaprojects in the city was accompanied with the destruction of previous buildings and landscapes and their replacement with a new built environment to enable the new, more innovative means of production and yield more profits. This section analyzes the study cases to find out what physical landscapes the process of creative destruction in Amman targeted, what power was exercised during this process, and how power relations played out in the transformation of the city's built environment. The second section, The Image, studies the megaprojects in terms of their image building. It argues that the production of a modern downtown, tall buildings, and spectacular developments was a means to create a new image for the city suitable for the new millennium. The third section, Commodified Spaces, shows how megaprojects in early twenty-first-century Amman were a significant example of producing the urban built environment, and the city, as a commodity for consumption. It discusses the agency of the different stakeholders in the commodification of the city, highlighting the role of Gulf capital flows in disseminating ideas, images, and consumption patterns dictated by capitalists' interest.

Chapter 3, Negotiating Identity in Contemporary Megaprojects, discusses the Jordanian identity as expressed in and created through recent megaprojects in Amman and as communicated through the discourses of the developers, particularly advertisement. This chapter investigates the relation between identity negotiation in megaprojects and the state, Gulf capital inflows, capitalist system of production, and different power relations in the city. The chapter argues that the new megaprojects in Amman constituted a significant part of the official construction of Jordanianness. Following the elements with reference to which state institutions constructed Jordan's official national identity, the discussion in this chapter is organized under four sections: The Tribal Jordanian, The Muslim Jordanian, The Arab Jordanian, and The Modern Jordanian. Each of these sections discusses the relevant element of identification and investigates how and why contemporary megaprojects in the city connected with or disconnected from this particular component of the Jordanian identity. The chapter argues that these developments were conceived to construct the city residents and Jordanians as technologically advanced and modern consumers, thus advancing the construction of Amman as a global city.

Chapter 4, Findings and Conclusion, discusses the principal findings of the book as they relate to the research questions and considers the implications of these findings for major theoretical concepts and understandings related to this study. This chapter also draws upon contemporary urban development processes and cases in globalizing Western and Middle Eastern cities to investigate the specificity or generality of the form and function of early twenty-first-century megaprojects in Amman, as well the processes that produced these developments. The chapter concludes with recommendations for future research pertaining to the topic of the current book.

Notes

1 I use the term "global" with quotes since Amman has always been subject to global forces, which makes it a globalizing city since its foundation. Cities undergoing transformations as a result of contemporary globalization processes have been referred to as global, globalized, and globalizing. I understand cities under contemporary globalization processes, including Amman, as globalizing cities, not global cities. Unlike the other terms, the term "globalizing" does not imply the existence of a certain scale against which the degree of "globalness" is measured or a fixed pattern that determines that a city has become global. I also take issue with the term "global city," which has its origins in theories that understand the globalness of the city in terms of global competitiveness primarily based on the city's global economic integration and international producer-services, and promote the global city as the best place for corporate businesses and upscale entertainment and living. Describing a city as "globalizing" better expresses the ongoing economic, sociocultural, and political transformations of that city under contemporary globalization processes. For more on these different terms, see Marcuse and van Kempen (2000).

2 I define the term "megaproject" as I use it in this book under the section Research Problem and Questions. As for "gated communities," they are groups of upscale houses and supporting amenities surrounded by walls with controlled entrances, which restrict access to people living in these houses and their guests.

3 Hanieh (2011) argues convincingly that the Gulf has always been an important part of global capitalism. He writes, "the global economy is part of the actual essence of the Gulf itself – the development of the global 'appears' through the development of the Gulf" (p. 16). For Hanieh, "the Gulf materialized as a concrete spatial region alongside, within, and through the making of the global economy" (p. 16).

4 The image of the city is subjective since it is in part how people perceive the city. Furthermore, it is likely that a city will have many images depending on who perceives this city. What concerns us most here is the image of Amman as we can understand from the views of the public, observation of the city's built environment, and analysis of relevant visual and textual material.

5 The old landlord-tenant legislation stipulates that tenants of unfurnished property can hold the lease of that property at the same rent rate they first leased the property; the landlord does not have the right to evacuate the tenants or raise the rent. This legislation is believed to have discouraged investment. The new

landlord-tenant law allows changes in rent rates for leases held after 2000; earlier leases are subject to phased rent increase (Oxford Business Group, 2009).

6 Jordan opposed US military intervention to liberate Kuwait after its invasion by Iraq.

7 Jordan has a small, service-based economy. The country's revenues depend largely on the export of labor. It also receives international and regional financial assistance from countries such as the United States and Arab Gulf states, as well as foreign direct investment, principally from Arab Gulf states (Knowles, 2005; Pfeifer, 2010; Schlumberger, 2002).

8 Historical sources use the term "Modern Amman" to refer to the city since the late nineteenth century.

9 According to The World Bank (n.d.), in 2007, the period around which construction activities in Amman peaked, Jordan had a per capita gross domestic product (GDP) of USD2,970. The average unemployment rate in Jordan during the 2000s was over 14 percent (Hanieh, 2013). The World Bank estimated the country's GDP in 2015 as USD4,940. It also classified Jordan as an upper middle income country.

10 Jordan is a monarchy that has a hereditary ruling system and quasi-absolute rule. Ben-Dor (2000) refers to such a system as an active monarchy, as opposed to the constitutional monarchies of Europe where the monarch's power is limited. Also see Halliday (2000).

11 Schlumberger (2002, p. 244) suggests that Jordan's economic system can be called "patrimonial capitalism," which he believes better describes "the hybrid combination of informal socio-political remnants of a former rentier economy which coexist in structural contradiction with the formal institutions and policies associated with a market economy [that is, a capitalist economy]." Rentier economy "is an economy where the substantial part of its revenue accrues from foreign sources and under the form of rent" (Knowles, 2005, p. 10). From its establishment to the late 1980s, Jordan was a rentier state. It mostly depended on international aid between 1921 and the late 1960s, and on remittances as well as regional and international financial assistance from the early 1970s to late 1980s (Knowles, 2005; Schlumberger, 2002). Despite the persistence of the significance of rents for the economy of Jordan today, rentierism is no longer a prominent characteristic of the economy of Jordan (Schlumberger, 2002).

12 This comment was made by a senior engineer working in the building construction sector in Abu Dhabi when he visited Amman for the first time. By the late 1990s, Abu Dhabi had taller buildings and more impressive large-scale developments than Amman.

13 A relatively high number of Jordanians hold degrees in engineering and architecture. In 2008, the number of architects and civil, electrical, and mechanical engineers registered in the Jordan Engineers Association (JEA) was 69,717 (Department of Statistics, 2009). Registration in JEA is required for any architect or engineer practicing in Jordan. It is likely that many Jordanian architects and engineers working abroad maintain their registration in JEA.

14 These areas were given on aerial photos of Amman from 1992 and 2010, which I obtained from the Royal Jordanian Geographic Centre in Amman in 2010. These areas are not to be confused with the geographical area of Greater Amman, which by 2007 was 1,662 square kilometers (GAM, 2008).

15 Mario Botta made this comment during a lecture he delivered at Amman City Hall on February 12, 2001, an event organized by the Center for the Study of the Built Environment (CSBE) in Amman.

16 Earlier publications on the Abdali development do not speak of Horizon; rather they speak of Oger Jordan, a subsidiary of the Saudi Arabia–based Saudi Oger (see Abdali Investment and Development, 2008). Saudi Oger was established by Rafik Hariri, the former prime minister of Lebanon. A few years after the death of Rafik Hariri, his son Bahaa left the Hariri-family Saudi Oger to establish Horizon Group.

17 The *dunum* is the unit for measuring land area in Jordan. One *dunum* equals 1,000 square meters.

18 Al Hamad Contracting Company was the contractor for Jordan Gate before becoming also a codeveloper of the project.

19 The size of the foundation hole is according to the developers' press release (see "Limitless digs," 2009).

References

Abdali Investment and Development (AID). (n.d.). Project fact sheet. Retrieved April 16, 2016, from http://www.abdali.jo/pdf/Factsheet-English.pdf.

Abdali Investment and Development (AID). (2008). *Abdali Newsletter, 4*. Retrieved August 10, 2016, from http://www.abdali.jo/images/albums/pdf/press_134090 028649.pdf.

Abdali Investment and Development (AID). (2010). Abdali, the Central Business District of Amman [obtained from AID].

Abdali Investment and Development (AID). (2015). The New Downtown of Amman. Retrieved March 26, 2016, from http://www.abdali.jo/pdf/abdali-2015. pdf.

Anderson, B. (2006; first published 1983). *Imagined communities: Reflections on the origin and spread of nationalism* (2nd ed.). London: Verso.

Ben-Dor, G. (2000). Patterns of monarchy in the Middle East. In J. Kostiner (Ed.), *Middle East monarchies: The challenge of modernity* (pp. 71–84). London: Lynne Rienner.

Creswell, J. (2007). *Qualitative inquiry & research design: Choosing among five approaches* (2nd ed.). Thousand Oaks, CA: Sage.

Damra, Y. M. (2009, December 3). Duyun Dubai al-'Alamiyya takshif ta'aththur tanfid mashru' Sanaya 'Amman al-tabi' li al-sharika [Dubai World's debt reveals hindrance in the execution of the Sanaya Amman project; in Arabic]. Retrieved August 10, 2016, from http://sahafi.jo/nsart_info.php?id=164cb52190d5488bca4 06fe86b1cf588f95cbf26.

Dean, M. (1999). *Governmentality: Power and rule in modern society*. London: Sage.

Department of Statistics (DOS). (2007). *Analytical report of multi-purpose household survey 2003*. Amman: Department of Statistics.

Department of Statistics (DOS). (2009). *Statistical yearbook, 2008*. Amman: Department of Statistics.

Department of Statistics (DOS). (2016). Taqrir al-nata'ij al-ra'isiyya lil ti'dad al-'am lil sukkan wa al-masakin 2015 [Report on main results of population and housing census 2015; in Arabic]. Retrieved June 25, 2016, from http://census.dos.gov.jo/ wp-content/uploads/sites/2/2016/02/Census_results_2016.pdf.

Dwairi, M. (2008, July 22). Itlaq a'mal al-bina' li abraj Sanaya 'Amman al-sakaniyya bi hajm istithmar 300 million dollar [Launch of construction work on the Sanaya

Amman residential towers with an investment size of 300 million dollars; in Arabic]. *Al Rai*, p. 26.

Elsheshtawy, Y. (Ed.). (2004). *Planning Middle Eastern cities: An urban kaleidoscope in a globalizing world*. New York: Routledge.

Elsheshtawy, Y. (Ed.). (2008). *The evolving Arab city: Tradition, modernity and urban development*. New York: Routledge.

Elsheshtawy, Y. (2010). *Dubai: Behind an urban spectacle*. New York: Routledge.

Foucault, M. (1969/1972). *The archaeology of knowledge and the discourse on language* (A. M. S. Smith, Trans.). London: Tavistock and New York: Pantheon Books.

Foucault, M. (1974/2007). *The incorporation of the hospital into modern technology* (E. K. Jr., W. King & S. Elden, Trans.). In J. Crampton & S. Elden (Eds.), *Space, knowledge and power: Foucault and geography* (pp. 141–151). Burlington, VT: Ashgate.

Foucault, M. (1975/1995). *Discipline and punish: The birth of the prison* (A. Sheridan, Trans. 2nd ed.). New York: Vintage Books.

Foucault, M. (1976/2003). Lecture two (D. Macey, Trans.). In M. Bertani & A. Fontana (Eds.), *Society must be defended: Lectures at the Collège de France, 1975–76*. New York: Picador.

Foucault, M. (1980). Questions on geography (C. Gordon, L. Marshall, J. Mepham, & K. Soper, Trans.). In C. Gordon (Ed.), *Power/knowledge: Selected interviews and other writings 1972–1977* (pp. 63–77). New York: Pantheon Books.

Foucault, M. (1984/2003). The ethics of the concern of the self as a practice of freedom. In P. Rabinow & N. Rose (Eds.), *The essential Foucault: Selections from the essential works of Foucault 1954–1984* (pp. 25–42). New York: New Press.

GFH's Jordan Gate project due for completion early 2011. (2010). Retrieved August 11, 2016, from http://www.zawya.com/mena/en/story/ZAWYA20100905073805/.

Greater Amman Municipality (GAM). (2007a). *High rise towers: An integral part of Amman's urban landscape* [CD]. Amman: Greater Amman Municipality.

Greater Amman Municipality (GAM). (2007b). *Corridor intensification strategy (CIS) development manual* [CD]. Amman: Greater Amman Municipality.

Greater Amman Municipality (GAM). (2008). *The Amman Plan: Metropolitan growth summary report* [CD]. Amman: Greater Amman Municipality.

Green, innovative and sustainable projects mark the success story of Limitless. (2009, April–May). *Real Estate & Investment: Middle East*, 28–30.

Gulf Finance House B.S.C. (2006–2007). *Jordan Land, 9*, 119–126.

Hall, P. (1998). *Cities in civilization*. New York: Pantheon Books.

Halliday, F. (2000). Monarchies in the Middle East: A concluding appraisal. In J. Kostiner (Ed.), *Middle East monarchies: The challenge of modernity* (pp. 289–303). London: Lynne Rienner.

Hanieh, A. (2011). *Capitalism and class in the Gulf Arab states*. New York: Palgrave Macmillan.

Hanieh, A. (2013). *Lineages of revolt: Issues of contemporary capitalism in the Middle East*. Chicago: Hypermarket Books.

Harvey, D. (1989). *The urban experience*. Baltimore: Johns Hopkins University Press.

Harvey, D. (1990). *The condition of postmodernity: An enquiry into the origins of cultural change*. New York: Blackwell.

Harvey, D. (1991). The urban face of capitalism. In J.F. Hart (Ed.), *Our changing cities* (pp. 51–66). Baltimore and London: Johns Hopkins University Press.

Harvey, D. (2001). The art of rent: Globalization and the commodification of culture. In *Spaces of capital: Towards a critical geography* (pp. 394–411). New York: Routledge.

Harvey, D. (2005). *The new imperialism*. Oxford: Oxford University Press.

Hazaimeh, H. (2007, August 28). Jordan Gate stands as tallest building in town. *The Jordan Times*, p. 1.

Hazaimeh, H. (2008, May 12). Kingdom to see more mega real estate projects. *The Jordan Times*, p. 1.

Hazaimeh, H. (2010, August 18). Deal allows construction to proceed at Jordan Gate towers. *The Jordan Times*, pp. 1, 5.

Henry, C.M., & Springborg, R. (2010). *Globalization and the politics of development in the Middle East* (2nd ed.). Cambridge, MA: Cambridge University Press.

Injaz 80% min Bawwabat al-Urdun wa ihtimam Khaliji bi al-suq al-Urduniyya [Completion of 80% of Jordan Gate and Gulf interest in the Jordanian market; in Arabic]. (2008, January 2). *Al Rai*.

Investment boom from Gulf petrodollars makes Jordanians leery their nation is being sold out. (2008, July 13). *Herald Tribune*.

Kanna, A. (Ed.). (2008). *The superlative city: Dubai and the urban condition in the early twenty-first century*. Cambridge, MA: Harvard University Press.

Kanna, A. (2011). *Dubai: The city as corporation*. Minneapolis: University of Minnesota Press.

Katz, C. (2006). Messing with 'the project'. In N. Castree & D. Gregory (Eds.), *David Harvey: A critical reader* (pp. 234–246). Oxford: Blackwell.

Khalaf, S. (2006). *Heart of Beirut: Reclaiming the Bourj*. London: Al Saqi Books.

Knowles, W. (2005). *Jordan since 1989: A study in political economy*. London and New York: I.B. Tauris.

Limitless digs deep to reach new heights in Jordan. (2009, March 2). Retrieved August 10, 2016, from http://limitless.com/en-gb/newsroom/02-03-2009/Limitless digs deep to reach new heights in Jordan.aspx.

Malkawi, S., & Kaddoura, H. (2007). *Ontology of Amman: Soul and body – study of the development of the Arab modern city* [in Arabic with a few sections translated into English]. Amman: Nara.

Marcuse, P., & van Kempen, R. (2000). Conclusion: A changed spatial order. In P. Marcuse & R. van Kempen (Eds.), *Globalizing cities: A new spatial order?* (pp. 249–275). Oxford: Blackwell.

Massad, J. (2001). *Colonial effects: The making of national identity in Jordan*. New York: Columbia University Press.

McDonough, T., Reich, M., & Kotz, D.M. (2010). Introduction: Social structure of accumulation theory for the 21st century. In T. McDonough, M. Reich, & D.M. Kotz (Eds.), *Contemporary capitalism and its crises: Social structure of accumulation theory for the 21st century* (pp. 1–19). New York: Cambridge University Press.

Namrouqa, H. (2016, May 23). Construction of Jordan Gate twin towers to resume after years of suspension. *The Jordan Times*. Retrieved July 7, 2016, from http://www.jordantimes.com/news/local/construction-jordan-gate-twin-towers-resume-after-years-suspension.

Oxford Business Group (OBG). (2008). *The report: Jordan 2008*. London: Oxford Business Group.

Oxford Business Group (OBG). (2009). *The report: Jordan 2009*. London: Oxford Business Group.

Oxford Business Group (OBG). (2010). *The report: Jordan 2010*. London: Oxford Business Group.

Parker, C. (2009). Tunnel-bypasses and minarets of capitalism: Amman as neoliberal assemblage. *Political Geography, 28*, 110–120.

Pfeifer, K. (2010). Social structure of accumulation theory for the Arab world: The economics of Egypt, Jordan, and Kuwait in the regional system. In T. McDonough, M. Reich, & D. M. Kotz (Eds.), *Contemporary capitalism and its crises: Social structure of accumulation theory for the 21st century* (pp. 309–353). New York: Cambridge University Press.

Queen Alia International Airport, Amman. (n.d.). Retrieved August 10, 2016, from http://www.fosterandpartners.com/projects/queen-alia-international-airport/.

Reuters. (2009). Nakheel, Limitless assets likely to be 'forced' to sell on Dubai World overhaul. *Saudi Gazette*. Retrieved August 11, 2016, from http://www.sauress.com/en/saudigazette/55892.

Reuters. (2010, June 29). Amman's new business core ready in Q1 2011 – developer. *The Daily Star*. Retrieved August 11, 2016, from http://www.dailystar.com.lb/Business/Middle-East/2010/Jun-29/85880-ammans-new-business-core-ready-in-q1-2011-developer.ashx.

Schlumberger, O. (2002). Jordan's economy in the 1990s: Transition to development? In G. Joffé (Ed.), *Jordan in transition* (pp. 225–253). New York: Palgrave Macmillan.

Sewel, W. H., Jr. (1992). A theory of structure: Duality, agency, and transformation. *American Journal of Sociology, 98*(1), 1–29.

Singerman, D., & Amar, P. (Eds.). (2006). *Cairo cosmopolitan: Politics, culture, and urban space in the new Middle East*. Cairo: American University of Cairo Press.

UAE firm to construct 60-storey twin towers in Abdoun. (2008, February 14). *The Jordan Times*.

United Nations – Economic and Social Commission for Western Asia. (2005). *Urbanization and the changing character of the Arab city* (Report No. E/ESCWA/SDD/2005/1). New York: United Nations.

Wad' hajar asas mashru' Bawwabat al-Urdun . . . al-yawm [Laying the cornerstone for the Jordan Gate project . . . today; in Arabic]. (2005, May 29). *Al Rai*.

Walter, N. (2010, July 27). Limitless forced to put majority of projects on hold. *Gulf News*. Retrieved August 10, 2016, from http://gulfnews.com/business/property/limitless-forced-to-put-majority-of-projects-on-hold-1.659863.

World Bank. (n.d.). GDP per capita – Jordan. Retrieved August 11, 2016, from http://data.worldbank.org/indicator/NY.GDP.PCAP.CD?locations=JO.

2 Constructing global Amman

Creative destruction

Following the theorization of Harvey (1989, 1990, 2005), urban transformation, particularly under contemporary globalization processes, can be understood in terms of capitalism's creative destruction. As capitalists look for more innovative means of production that will yield more profits, they destroy the built environment they produced previously in order to replace it with a new built environment that enables the new innovation. This process of creative destruction was pertinent in the context of urban transformations in Amman's built environment in the early twenty-first century. A close look at megaprojects carried out in the city in this period reveals what physical landscapes the process of creative destruction in Amman targeted, what power was exercised during this process, and how power relations played out in the transformation of the city's built environment.

For The New Downtown of Amman (Abdali), Jordan Gate, and Sanaya Amman to take place, buildings and landscapes already on the sites of the future projects had to be torn down. The site of the Abdali development primarily included military facilities and the Central Intelligence Agency buildings. When these buildings were built in the 1960s and 1970s, this site had not yet become the center of Amman, and it was appropriate at that time to locate state institutions such as the military at the margins of the city. Although the site became the center of the city in the 1980s, it continued to accommodate the military and other relevant state institutions, as the condition that produced such state buildings remained largely unchanged. Both the defensive and, at times, repressive functions of the institutions occupying these buildings continued to be relevant through the 1980s. At the turn of the millennium, however, the condition under which military buildings in Abdali were produced had changed. The state signed a peace treaty with Israel in 1994, and modernization processes were underway. The state was no longer at war, and as a sign of adopting modernization and the democratic processes the state's defensive and repressive apparatus were shifted away from the center of the city. Thus, the site could be cleared for redevelopment. In addition to the state-owned buildings, the process of creative destruction targeted privately owned residential, commercial, and educational buildings on the site of the future Abdali project.

Creative destruction in the context of Jordan Gate targeted the public park on the site of this development. The creation of the park by Greater Amman Municipality (GAM) early in the last quarter of the twentieth century was appropriate to this particular moment of time. The land of the park, which constituted the prime cost of this park, was donated by privileged city residents. The park can be understood as an investment in the Sixth Circle area, then a suburban area of Western Amman. By enhancing the quality of space in this area, GAM encouraged city residents to move into this western part of the city. This, in turn, relieved the crowded areas in the rest of the city, created demand for land in Western Amman, encouraged construction, and stimulated the city's economy. By the early twenty-first century, the Sixth Circle area had become one of Western Amman's affluent areas. At the same time, developers from the Gulf states were looking for investment in urban developments in the city. New opportunities emerged for GAM to make profit through the transformation of the park into a mixed-use megaproject. Thus, the structures and landscapes in the park were demolished so that the developers could produce the new development, which when completed would be more profitable than the park.

At Sanaya Amman, creative destruction targeted the natural landscape. This process was different than that in the previous cases because the landscape of the Sanaya site was destroyed but the buildings that were supposed to replace this landscape and produce profit for the developers and the city were never built. Although losses were incurred, there were no gains as in Abdali or expected future gains as in Jordan Gate. The developers failed to realize their project and the anticipated earnings. GAM, however, made some profit by selling this site to the developers, after it managed to change building regulation in the area to allow such a large-scale high-rise development to take place. Still, GAM did not accomplish the long-term gain it expected from the creative destruction process that targeted this site.

Yielding profit was the primary concern for the developers of Amman's contemporary megaprojects. Investing in the urban built environment in Amman was seen as a means to economic development integral to the modernization campaign the state launched in the early twenty-first century. Here, the Abdali development is a telling example. Mawared, the state-owned developers in the AID joint venture that developed The New Downtown, found developing the site into a large-scale mixed-use megaproject the best way to produce profit. Thus, officials at Mawared talked about how the site of the Abdali development was a "prime land" that should be invested

(M. Rihani, personal communication, August 16, 2010). It turned out that the plans for this development would change more than once over the course of time as more profitable development opportunities emerged. A significant part of the Abdali development was to accommodate the American University of Amman (Dwairi, 2005). Many in Amman were optimistic about this development because an educational institution such as this could have benefited the city and given its higher education institutions, already well respected in the region, an edge over other cities. However, as more profitable options for development emerged, the university proposal was abandoned to be replaced with commercial buildings. One cannot but wonder how a decision regarding the establishment of a university at the center of the city could have changed in a matter of a couple of years. It might be expected that such a decision would have been based on an extensive study of the needs of the city residents. But this was not the case. The Abdali's principal purpose was profit making rather than fulfilling the city residents' needs.

This was also evident in another plan change for the Abdali development. Earlier Abdali plans and documents included a cultural component at the eastern end of the Abdali site, which would have connected the Abdali project with the state buildings: King Abdullah I Mosque, the Parliament, and the Court of Law (see Abdali Investment and Development [AID], n.d.a, pp. 13–14; Dwairi, 2005).[1] These plans referred to this cultural component of the project as the Abdali development's cultural or civic pole, which included a library, a museum, and a plaza. But commercial buildings replaced these service buildings and spaces. It turned out, according to the planners of this development, that no government institution would fund the building of the cultural component at the Abdali development (R. Abou Rayan, personal communication, August 2 and 8, 2010). Instead, the developers, including the state-owned Mawared, preferred to invest in more profitable components of this project, particularly in entertainment and shopping spaces.

Decision-making regarding the production of Amman's megaprojects followed a top-down approach. This was obvious in the planning process for the development of the site of the future New Downtown, where the public had no voice in the largest development in contemporary Amman, a development that would dramatically change a central area of the city. Commenting on this approach, a planner and architect in Amman said that it was common in the country. The prevailing assumption was that experts were better qualified than the people – those most affected by the project – to decide. There were a number of ways the Abdali site could have been developed to benefit Amman residents, but little input was sought from them. Professionals in fields relating to architecture and urban planning who had no conflict of interest in relation to this project, including regionally renowned Jordanian architect Rasem Badran, suggested that the site should have been developed into a public park that would have served as the lungs of the increasingly crowded city, which lacked open public spaces (personal communication, September 1, 2010). In fact, internal sources mentioned that one of the scenarios briefly considered for the development of the Abdali site was its transformation into a public park. However, it soon became obvious that any development that would not yield profit was out of the question.

This was the same logic that led to the demolition of the park on the site of the future Jordan Gate development. In this case not only were the needs of the community ignored but also the legal consequences for transforming land that was donated for the purpose of creating a park into a commercial development. The place where neighborhood residents, as well as other city residents, entertained, socialized, and played games was to be transformed into an upscale development that primarily catered to the affluent segment of the society and promoted consumption. GAM made the decision to develop the park as a top-down decision with no public participation. The GAM committee consisted of planners, architects, business persons, among others. According to a committee insider, of the forty members who voted, only seven voted against the Jordan Gate development. City officials and the committee were lured by the profit GAM could make as a partner in this development. Thus, GAM became both the legislator and a beneficiary from this development, as GAM officials would admit a few years later ("Ittifaqiyyat bay'," 2007). No wonder that building regulations, particularly as they related to building heights, were skewed in favor of the developers and certain licensing processes were bypassed.

In both the Abdali and Jordan Gate developments, some city residents contested the power of corporate developers to destroy built environments that already existed on the sites and replace them with the new projects. In the case of Abdali, this was obvious in the public's response to the transfer of ownership of properties on the site. True at times, the transition of ownership to the developers went smoothly as property owners were lured by the generous amounts the Abdali developers offered them or were intimidated by the power of these developers. But at other times, the process involved a battle between property owners who refused to sell their properties and the developers who needed these properties to execute their plans, which had been completed before securing ownership of the site. The case of Talal Abu-Ghazaleh Organization (TAG-Org) became very famous in Amman. TAG-Org exercised its power to destabilize the otherwise hegemonic power of the developers. When TAG-Org refused to sell its property on the Abdali site to AID, GAM put forward plans for a new public park and a street that would cut through this property (Kayyali, 2008). Consequently, GAM was able to expropriate this property on the basis that it would be used for the public good. GAM then sold the property to AID who soon after demolished TAG-Org's buildings to realize its plans for The New Downtown. TAG-Org filed a case against GAM, claiming that the expropriation of its property was invalid and unfair, but they lost (Kayyali, 2008; also see "'Abu-Ghazaleh' tarfud," 2006; "Majmu'at Abu-Ghazaleh," 2007).

Like TAG-Org, the public, particularly residents in the neighborhood of Jordan Gate, who were outraged by GAM's decision to transform the park and by the scale of this development exercised their power. Consequently, a campaign was launched against the Jordan Gate development. Although the campaign was small, it was significant in the context of Amman where it was unlikely that the public would take to the streets for matters relating to the built environment in the city. At the time, Jordan's democratic processes were new, untested, and far from complete. The original donors of the park's land, according to professionals and others interviewed over the course of this research, objected the transformation of the park into a commercial megaproject, taking their case to court. Sources said that consequently these donors received monetary compensation. The campaign and the court case against Jordan Gate might have shaken those in charge of this development, but they could not stop it. One immediate outcome was that the mayor of Amman under whom Jordan Gate took place was asked to step down. The new mayor sold GAM's share in this development to a private Gulf-state developer, Bayan Holding (Hazaimeh, 2007; "Ittifaqiyyat bay'," 2007). The mayor wanted to revoke the building license of Jordan Gate and asked the developers to reduce the height of the buildings (Al-Wazani, 2006), but in the end, the development continued as planned.

Jordan Gate was produced at the expense of the public. Residents of this development's neighborhood, as well as those who worked there, passed through the area, or visited it had to adjust to new situations, whether traffic congestion, lack of parking space, or the loss of a much appreciated open public space in the area. Almost everyone I interviewed who lived or worked in the neighborhood of Jordan Gate, as well as many individuals who visited the neighborhood frequently, talked about how the park served the local community and people of Western Amman. Adil talked passionately about the park and the small soccer field that existed there (personal communication, September 29, 2010).[2] He said, "I, my friends, and other neighbors used to form teams and compete against each other. Those were great times." Kareema talked about the park's indoor skating rink (personal communication, September 28, 2010). She said, "the building that hosted the rink was modest, but it was spacious and nice and my children and I had fun there." Atif talked about how much he liked pine trees in the park and spoke sadly about their clear-cutting in preparation for the new development (personal communication, September 28, 2010). Atif said, "now that the park is closed, I have to drive my children to a park far from home. But we don't go as often." Hassan talked about how he used to go to the park with his wife and children after work (personal communication, August 2010). They would play or take a walk then have some sandwiches; sometimes they met with other friends there. Clearly, the park was a breathing space for people in the neighborhood and the surrounding areas. It was a place for leisure, relaxation, and socialization, a much needed space that is missed.

As in the case of Jordan Gate, the demolition of buildings and urban spaces on the site of the future New Downtown had negative consequences for residents of the Abdali neighborhood, as well as other city residents. Those who lived, worked, or went to school there had to take longer and more expensive trips to school or work, but that cost did not detract from the benefits accrued to the developers. Along with the destruction of previous buildings on the site and the relocation of those who once occupied it, good and bad memories associated with this site were fading. Today, many young adults in the city identify the site only with the Abdali development.

The preceding discussion shows that regardless of the developer or whether or not the development was undertaken as a public-private partnership, The New Downtown, Jordan Gate, and Sanaya Amman were conceived within the capitalist logic of production and its creative destruction. The power of corporations, the state, and the city was dominant in these developments, although it was sometimes contested by micro-powers such as those exercised by groups of the public in the context of the Abdali and Jordan Gate developments. It was primarily profit-making that drove the production of contemporary megaprojects in Amman, not the needs of the city residents. Amman's megaprojects also showed how decision-makers in the city were desperate to chase capital flows from the Gulf states. Decision-makers viewed megaprojects as investment opportunities that would strengthen the city's as well as the country's economy, not least through transforming the image of the city.

The image

Under contemporary globalization processes and the logic of capital associated with these processes, image building became an important form of investment. Imaging or constructing an image of the urban built environment through the production of buildings and landscapes of certain characteristics that created the built environment as a distinguished place for living, work, and entertainment proved profitable. Producing spectacular urban spaces became a common practice. Thus, developers produced splendid developments to enhance their corporate image and increase their profits, and architects designed such developments to boost their portfolio.

Similarly, city officials became concerned with city imaging as a means to market and sell places and buttress their city's economy (see Harvey, 1990, 2001a, 2001b). Focusing on creating the image of developments and the city, corporations and officials disregarded the needs of the city's working- and middle-class residents. The large scale, high visibility, high cost, and anticipated high profit from megaprojects made them a good means through which to create a city image. Thus in early twenty-first-century Amman, megaprojects were used to re-image the city or project a new image for Amman. But what image did these megaprojects seek to construct and how did they construct this image?

The developers of The New Downtown and their planners were explicit about the significance of image building in the conception of this development. The Abdali project was designed to create an image integral to the new image of Amman and the city's, as well as Jordan's, economic development (see Figure 1.2). Thus in the regulations for this project, the developers stated that one of the "principal indicators" for the assessment of the impact of Abdali on the city's and country's economy was its creation of an "improved image of Amman" (AID, n.d.a, p. 4). A key goal of Abdali as stated in these regulations was "to develop a vibrant, tightly knit, architecturally distinctive, and modern urban nucleus that [would change] the past image of the site and [become] a pole of excellence attracting the best talents to live, study, work, and entertain" (AID, n.d.a, p. 2). The developers of The New Downtown believed it would "catapult the city of Amman into the 21st century, placing it at [*sic*] par with most renowned cities of the world" and "provoking an unprecedented influx of investments from Jordan and the region" (AID, 2010). It is in light of this role of Abdali that the extensive advertisement accompanying the project can be understood. Thus the advertisements that used to be posted on the enormous construction fence that encircled the site included phrases such as "let us welcome the world," which presented Abdali as a gateway to the world, as a regional and global development, not merely a local or national project. Obviously, the Abdali developers sought a modern image for the project that would make Amman a global city.

Similarly, the developers of Jordan Gate praised the appearance of this development (see Figure 1.6), referring to it as a "masterpiece of architecture" that was a quality addition to Amman ("(Al Hamad) tunjiz," 2006). The image of this development would translate into a profit ("GFH's Jordan Gate," 2010), attracting investors to Amman ("Jordan Gate breaks ground," 2005), helping transform the city into a world business destination ("Janahi: 40% al-injaz," 2007), and boosting the country's economy ("Janahi: 40% al-injaz," 2007; "Jordan Gate breaks ground," 2005). The advertisements speak of Jordan Gate as an "architecture expression" of the country's growing economy, an energizer for the country, and a new start for Jordan (Bayan Holding, Gulf Finance House, & Kuwait Finance & Investment Company, 2007, 2007–2008; Jordan Gate Company, n.d.). The mayor of Amman, under whom Jordan Gate was begun as a partnership between GAM and Gulf states' developers, said that this development would be a distinctive contribution to Amman's built environment, serving as a distinguished tourist destination, encouraging foreign investment, and enhancing the city's economy ("Wad' hajar," 2005). Like the developers of Abdali, Jordan Gate's developers sought an image for their project that would contribute to the construction of global Amman.

A modern downtown

A visitor to the city in the early twenty-first century criticized the original downtown of Amman (Figure 2.1) saying that "it lack[ed] most of the attributes of a downtown: [t]he bright lights, shops, sights and attractions" (Mumtaz, 2006, para. 5). According to this visitor, he passed through the downtown without realizing it. These comments reflected the status of the downtown at that time. This is not to say that downtown Amman has turned into a deserted area. In fact, it is still busy, and sometimes overcrowded, on weekends and on weekday mornings and afternoons, but not as busy at night. However, anyone who visits the downtown or passes through it will realize that it is no longer the place that brings together people from all segments of Amman's society. Instead, the downtown mostly serves working-class residents of the city. Many Ammanis rarely pass through the downtown, let alone shop or wander in it (see Al-Asad, 2008; Malkawi & Kaddoura, 2007); a situation that traces back to the 1970s when many government and corporate offices as well as commercial facilities moved out to new western sections of Amman (United Nations, 2005), but became more obvious in the following decades. By the end of the first decade of the twenty-first century, GAM had begun renovation work on downtown Amman in an effort to make it more attractive, particularly to tourists.[3]

Given the status of the original downtown of Amman in the early 2000s, the developers and state thought its replacement with the new Abdali was legitimate. By itself, the name "The New Downtown of Amman" constructs the Abdali development as the replacement for the city's downtown, as the new place where city residents will shop, socialize, and entertain and major businesses and commercial facilities will be located. For the Abdali developers, referring to this development as The New Downtown is a means to emphasize the significance of Abdali and its central location and, consequently, attract more investors, prospective property buyers, businesses, tourists, and city residents, thus increasing the developers' profit. For the state, this name

Figure 2.1 View of downtown Amman on a weekend afternoon.
Note: Taken by the author on October 15, 2010.

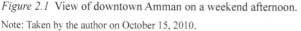

means Jordan can claim that its capital city has a downtown similar to downtowns in modern and global cities, a downtown that can support regional and international businesses and host activities similar to those hosted in the downtowns of other prominent cities. Such a downtown will enhance the image of Amman, attracting businesses and individuals along with their capital and money, not least through the collective image it projects.

Thus whereas the developers of Jordan Gate and Sanaya Amman were concerned with creating images of individual developments, the Abdali developers were concerned with imaging a whole district as can be inferred from the design concept of The New Downtown and its building regulations. Describing the plans of the Abdali development, the developers wrote, "view corridors form[ed] the main composition lines of the project" (AID, n.d.a, p. 7). These corridors, according to the developers, converged toward state buildings located east of the Abdali development. It was these "view corridors" that "guide[d] the alignment of streets and the placement of high [rise] buildings" (AID, n.d.a, p. 7). Not only was the image of the Abdali development important but also the images seen from this development.

Thus, it was important for the planners that "building form . . . [be] directed toward allowing . . . views into local areas rather than blocking them" (AID, n.d.a, p. 7). This recalled modern planning principles – inherited from the Baroque urban aesthetic – as manifested in the Haussmannian Paris (1853–1870) where buildings and spaces were organized with emphasis on the image and vista. Haussmann's planning model in turn influenced planning practices in colonial and postcolonial Arab Middle Eastern cities in the late nineteenth and twentieth centuries. Beirut is one such city and, interestingly, the architects and planners of Abdali – LACECO – were based in Beirut and took part in the planning of one of the city's largest developments in the 1990s, Beirut Central District (BCD). Also the developers of the BCD were closely connected, particularly at an early stage of the Abdali development, to Horizon, one of the developers in the joint venture of AID. In fact, Makdisi (1997) found that the appearance of the BCD was most important in the conception of this project.

The significance of the image for the Abdali development was obvious in the ways building shapes were controlled. Building regulations described the urban and architectural character of The New Downtown to which developers should adhere (Abdali Mall Company [AMC], 2007; AID, n.d.a; AID, 2006). These regulations, according to the Abdali planners and architects, were derived from old buildings in Amman, particularly in the downtown, and developments in neighboring cities, such as Beirut Central District. Buildings in Abdali were required to adhere to a tripartite organization consisting of building base, body, and top, and each of these parts was regulated in terms of its design and accents used to emphasize the different parts of the building (AMC, 2007; AID, n.d.a; AID, 2006). Interestingly, old buildings in Amman were known for having no distinctive top. To allow for vertical expansion, columns more often than not extended around 50cm above the roof; and the last floor was never treated as such because it was kept in mind that it might one day become a middle floor. There are different theoretical understandings of the tripartite composition of buildings. One of these is that it is a persisting influence of high-rise buildings in the late nineteenth and early twentieth centuries in which the use of tripartite composition reflected the spirit of classical architecture through the allusion to the three components of the classical order: the pedestal, column, and entablature (see Summerson, 1963). Another understanding is that advanced by Louis Sullivan in the late nineteenth century, in which he attributed the tripartite division of the high-rise buildings he designed to the three different functions the building served. Following Sullivan's aphorism "form follows function," the commercial base, typical office floors, and the attic that housed mechanical equipment were to have distinguished forms (Mallgrave, 2005, p. 280).

The Abdali planners and architects regulated the solid-to-void ratio on the façades of this development's buildings so as it would be similar to the ratio in Amman's old buildings (AID, n.d.a; AID, 2006; AMC, 2007). But, maintaining such a ratio did not necessarily result in buildings with character similar to that of old buildings. Thus, more often than not the shape of the buildings in the Abdali development turned out different from old buildings in downtown Amman or in the Abdali neighborhood. Compare, for example, buildings in Figure 2.1 to those in Figure 2.2. Some buildings at the Abdali development, such as the buildings in Figure 2.3, can be seen as hybrid, combining new and old architectural vocabulary and materials – glass curtain walls, stone-clad walls, and small windows.

Although the rhetoric of AID and LACECO seemed to show respect for old buildings in Amman, the developers and their architects and planners were keen to differentiate the Abdali development from these buildings. This was obvious even in their regulation for building finishing. On the one hand, to keep with "the spirit" of old buildings in the immediate context of the Abdali development, stone was required as the main finishing material (AID, n.d.a, p. 48). On the other, to distinguish the Abdali development from its surrounding, warm yellow stone was to be used; and white stone commonly used on buildings in the neighborhood was "prohibited" (AID, n.d.a, p. 49). Similarly, rough-textured stone commonly used on older buildings in Amman, such as stone locally referred to as *mufajjar* and *tubzah*, was not

Figure 2.2 View of commercial buildings in the Abdali development from the street bordering this development on the south.

Note: Taken by May Musa on July 15, 2016.

Figure 2.3 View of small-scale developments along the southern edge of the Abdali development.

Note: Taken by May Musa on July 15, 2016.

allowed on buildings in the Abdali development. Instead, stone was to be smoothly finished (AID, n.d.a).

Building shapes in The New Downtown also were controlled through details and illustrated examples for different architectural elements, such as window shapes and proportions and canopy shapes, materials, and colors, included in the regulations for this development. The examples were primarily from Amman and Beirut, and included modern and postmodern styles. They even included sketch designs for the developments at different locations in Abdali showing how AID expected the buildings to look. The regulations for the Abdali development encouraged the use of double-skin façades (AID, n.d.a). Such façades would consist of an internal skin made of clear glass, and an external skin located up to 75cm from the internal skin and made of glass, stone, and wooden or metal louvers, among others. LACECO already used this approach in their designs for Beirut Central District where façades of historic buildings on the site were kept while the interiors of these buildings were remodeled, reducing these buildings to mere envelopes and projecting a historic image for this part of the development (see Saliba, 2007). The situation was different in The New Downtown where there were no historic buildings that needed façade preservation through the use of double skin. However, the double skin made it easier to control the image of Abdali, which in this case was a modern image.

To further ensure that aesthetic quality of buildings in The New Downtown was controlled, AID requested the developers of the different parcels to submit the designs of their buildings, including conceptual, preliminary, and final designs, for AID's approval (AID, 2006). The developers also were required to submit detailed designs of façades, including windows, sun shade devices, balconies, flower beds, balustrades, and canopies as well as samples of exterior finishing. This strict regulation of buildings' shape, material, and details paid off, producing high-quality buildings, as observation of this project showed and architects in the city noted. However, this regulation sometimes resulted in architects copying the examples of designs and details that the architects and planners of the Abdali development provided as a LACECO insider commented. The resulting similarity of the small-scale buildings along the Abdali development's southern edge (Figure 2.3) might be attributed, at least partly, to the control of the Abdali development's image through AID's strict regulation and extensive details and design examples, particularly for small-scale developments.

Tall buildings

High-rise buildings were among the most important image-constructing components in The New Downtown, Jordan Gate, and Sanaya Amman (see Figures 1.2, 1.6, and 1.8). Under contemporary globalization, tall buildings became a symbol of globality. The developers of contemporary megaprojects in Amman were well aware of that. The symbolic capital, which is transformable to money capital, associated with record-breaking tall buildings engendered competition for building the tallest building in Amman in the early twenty-first century. Thus, the unrealized Sanaya Amman (50 stories high and 200 meters tall) was designed to beat the record set by Jordan Gate (44 stories high and 150 meters tall). And Rotana Hotel in Abdali (50 stories high and 185 meters tall) was constructed to beat Jordan Gate just as the latter was constructed to beat the record set by Le Royal, which at 33 stories stood as the tallest building in Amman since its completion in 2003.

The developers of Abdali and Jordan Gate referred to tall buildings at these developments as landmarks. Lynch (1960, p. 48) defines the landmark as a "point-reference," a "simply defined physical object," which can be singled out from "a host of possibilities." Buildings can serve as landmarks "seen from many angles and distances" (p. 48). Lynch conceived landmarks as an important element in the design of "imageable" cities – legible cities where people moving around can easily identify physical structure and compose a mental image that helps them, among other things, navigate in the city (p. 10). Lynch's understanding of landmarks was different from the Abdali and Jordan Gate developers' conception of landmarks as

spectacular upscale developments to project an image of these developments and Amman, which would serve corporate developers rather than the
majority of the city residents.

Abdali was conceived with high-rise office buildings and hotels in the
IT Sector – the area at the western end of this development. Ranging in
height between 125 and 220 meters, these were planned and designed
as state-of-the-art buildings to serve as "*the* [emphasis added] landmark"
(AID, n.d.a, p. 22) of The New Downtown and Amman. These buildings,
according to the developers, also would serve as a "landmark of the new
economy of Amman" (p.12). The landmark buildings were placed on the
western side of the Abdali site not least because it provided "the highest
visibility" for these buildings, which conformed to the significant role
of the IT Sector in projecting "the new business image of the country"
(AID, n.d.a, p. 22). High-rise buildings at Abdali were not restricted to
the IT Sector. Although today The New Downtown has only a handful
of tall buildings, plans for Abdali included no less than 20 tall buildings
proposed for the site at different locations. Sources interviewed over
the course of this research indicated that in the 2000s when a developer
showed interest in developing parcels in the project's site as a high-rise
building, plans were changed to accommodate demands of this developer.
However, the Abdali developers' justification for high-rise buildings at
the Abdali development was that these buildings were carefully located
to "mark certain areas as critical anchors," "define gateways to the Abdali
District," and serve as landmarks (AMC, 2007, p. 11). So proud were the
Abdali developers of this development's tall buildings and the image
they created that they strongly emphasized and even exaggerated them in
the early renderings and advertisements of this project. Thus one of the
earliest and most circulated advertisements of Abdali, "The Downtown
Comes Soaring to Life," primarily consisted of a 3D view of The New
Downtown dominated by high-rise buildings with glittering surfaces tow-
ering over the surrounding urban fabric of the Abdali neighborhood (Figure 2.4). This advertisement's title and text also indicated the great stature
of the development's buildings. To make sure that the message was clear
to the audiences of this advertisement, the developers elsewhere proudly
described the buildings in the Abdali development as they appeared in the
image of this advertisement as "rising tall" over the surrounding urban
fabric ("Abdali PSC launches," 2008).

For the developers of Sanaya Amman, the twin towers were a means
to create an "iconic development" ("Green, innovative," 2009, p. 29). As
Sklair (2010, p. 143) points out, "recognition of the outline of a building, especially in a skyline, is one of the great signifiers of iconicity." In
architecture, iconicity is "fame and special symbolic/aesthetic significance
as applied to buildings, spaces and in some cases architects themselves"

The downtown comes soaring to life. Witness its rise.

www.abdali.jo

A new era begins with Abdali, the new downtown of Amman. 1,810,000 sqm of built-up area advancing to become a comprehensive center both modern and integrated. On every level, Abdali speaks developments, setting new foundations for business excellence through the introduction of 'smart' urban buildings supported by state of the-art technology, establishing it as the business hub of the future. With inspired design and upscale facilities Abdali sets new standards of living, flanking high-rise contemporary luxury apartments with diversified shopping districts that sparkle with global brands.

Live the vision

Figure 2.4 Advertisement of the Abdali development featuring tall buildings tower-
ing over the surroundings (2008).

Note: Reprinted with permission from Abdali Investment and Development and Leo Burnett Jordan.

(p. 135). Iconic buildings, as Cuadra (2007, p. 76) defines them, are "build-ings of an extremely powerful formal appearance." Iconic buildings and developments have a symbolic capital that can be transformed into money capital. Under contemporary globalization and the increasing competition between cities and within cities to capture capital, iconic developments emerged as a significant means of transforming the urban built environment, re-imaging places, and boosting the economy. It is not surprising then that the developers of Sanaya, who were but one of many transnational invest-ment corporations involved in developments in Amman in the early twenty-first century, emphasized the iconicity of Sanaya, particularly its impressive height, in their discourse. One of the most telling examples of the pride the Sanaya developers took in the grandness of this project was the advertise-ment titled "Sanaya Amman" featuring a 3D view of Sanaya supposedly placed in context. The landscape of the city appeared unrealistically flat and monotonous for the hilly city of Amman, consisting of low-rise buildings above which Sanaya towers. But, as Dovey (1999, p. 108) puts it, "advertis-ing portrays an ideal rather than a reality; it distorts as it mythologizes." The developers distorted the context of Sanaya and dwarfed the surrounding buildings to further emphasize this development's distinctive height. Such a distortion of the context of the advertised development and the domination of the context by the advertised buildings were an advertising strategy many developers in Amman and other cities around the world adopted to make their developments stand out and boost their symbolic capital, which is, as Dovey points out, the rationale behind the ubiquity of corporate towers in cities around the world. Thus Limitless stressed that Sanaya would be "the tallest building in the country and among the highest twin buildings in the Middle East," and it would have "the world's highest suspended swimming pool" ("$300m Limitless Towers," 2008). The developers were proud to emphasize the role this project would play in "reshaping the skyline" of Wadi Abdoun and Amman ("Limitless: Sanaya," n.d.).

If Sanaya was located in a wadi that had one of the lowest elevations in Amman, Jordan Gate occupied a site that had one of the highest elevations in the city. Furthermore, Jordan Gate was the first development and most likely the last of such a height in the area, since in 2007 the Amman Plan prohibited high-rise buildings in the neighborhood of Jordan Gate as well as in the surrounding areas (GAM, 2007). Thus, the Jordan Gate development in the early twenty-first century stood oddly in a surrounding urban fabric of low- to medium-rise buildings; it could be seen almost from anywhere in Amman (see Figures 1.1 and 2.5). According to Jafar Tukan (n.d., p. 3), the development's principal architect who was one of two prominent old-generation architects in Jordan, this added to the "uniqueness" of Jordan Gate. But many in Amman agreed that Jordan Gate had a negative impact on the city's skyline. Even Tukan spoke about how this development disrupted the skyline of the city and was reported to have said that following the construction of Jordan Gate, GAM took measures that would ensure there would be no further urban disharmony as that caused by Jordan Gate (Shamma, 2010). When asked why then the Consolidated Consultants-Jafar Tukan Architects undertook the design of this development, Tukan responded, "towers are a matter of reality necessitated by economic forces, not just an option on the table" (p. 36).

But many individuals interviewed over the course of this research were concerned about the intrusion of high-rise buildings on the city's skyline and wished the skyline of Amman was respected. Rasem Badran, the other prominent old-generation architect in Jordan, disagreed with Tukan's justification for undertaking the Jordan Gate project. He described Jordan Gate as a joke – "*mahzala*," to use his exact word – adding that if he had been in Tukan's shoes he would not have undertaken the designs for this project (personal communication, September 1, 2010). Other city residents criticized Jordan Gate's extreme height, particularly when compared to its surroundings, referring to it as an urban disaster that damaged the city's skyline. Similarly, many individuals commented on the image of the advertisement "The Downtown Comes Soaring to Life" (see Figure 2.4) and similar rendering of the Abdali development by saying they were disrespectful of the

Figure 2.5 View of the Jordan Gate development and its surroundings from a building on Mecca Street in Western Amman.

Note: Taken by May Musa on August 21, 2016.

city's skyline. Some blogged about the negative influence Sanaya Amman could have had on the city's landscape and its skyline. For example a blogger wrote, "Amman's hills are a precious asset and a hallmark of its identity. They are the 'icon' of Amman, and we really don't need new 'icons' that destroy its fabric and skyline" ("This insane skyscraper," 2009).

High-rise buildings of contemporary megaprojects in Amman and the image they project reflect the influence of Gulf states' developers and urbanism in Gulf cities, particularly Dubai, which architects and architectural historians in Amman have also pointed out (Al-Asad, 2007; R. Badran, personal communication, September 1, 2010). After all, Dubai is a city that is home to many iconic high-rise buildings and, more important, the tallest building in the world, Burj Khalifa (completed 2009), which made it a tourist destination and earned it a global reputation. Furthermore, several projects for tall buildings planned for Amman in the early 2000s – although not necessarily realized – were by Dubai-based developers, including Limitless and DAMAC. The influence of Dubai's architecture also can be traced in Jordan Gate, which had a design program similar to the program of Dubai's iconic Emirates Towers (completed 2000) – an office tower, a hotel tower, and a shopping mall connecting the two buildings. In fact, a few individuals interviewed for my research pointed out this similarity between the two developments. Both Jordan Gate and Emirates Towers are clad in modern glittering materials – the former is finished in glass, and the latter in aluminum panels and glass. At 56 and 54 stories, however, the Emirates Towers development is taller than Jordan Gate, and in 2000 it was the tallest not only in Dubai but in the Middle East and Europe (see Al-Asad, 2012).

The agency of the state and city in the production of Amman's new tall buildings and construction of the city image cannot be overemphasized. In the case of Jordan Gate, GAM bypassed building regulations, allowing the development of this high-rise project. In the Abdali development, the state-owned Mawared, which partnered with the corporate developers, facilitated investment in high-rise buildings. The plans for the Abdali project preceded GAM's designation of The New Downtown as one of the areas in the city where high-rise buildings were permitted. Thus, high-rise buildings were allowed in Abdali not because GAM deemed it was a suitable location for high-rise buildings, but because the Abdali developers, including Mawared, had already decided to invest in tall buildings in the area. GAM was the facilitator for the development of The New Downtown through its involvement in rearranging the road network in the surroundings of this project to allow for the heavy traffic this project would cause. GAM also interfered in favor of the developers, AID, in the case of Talal Abu-Ghazaleh Organization mentioned earlier, helping AID realize the image they sought for Abdali.

GAM was a powerful agent in the conception of Sanaya Amman, changing building regulations to allow high-rise buildings in the wadi where Sanaya was located (GAM, 2008a). GAM officials even designated the site of Sanaya, which GAM owned, for the tallest of the high-rise buildings in the area, inviting bidders for the site development. According to GAM officials, the designation of the wadi for tall buildings was made following careful studies that paid close attention to the city's urban fabric (B. Haddaden & R. Odeh, personal communications, July 15 and 21, 2010; also see "Mayor Omar," 2009). GAM believed the city needed high-rise buildings (Maani, 2007). For GAM, high-rise buildings were an "essential component of thriving, modern cities" (p. 12). High-rise buildings, according to GAM, "address[ed] real and emerging market demands and [met] the interest of investors" (p. 12). Thus, GAM in the early twenty-first century wanted to "Partner with Tower Investors" (p. 12). GAM's justification for allowing high-rise buildings in areas such as the site of Sanaya was that these buildings were "least disruptive" in wadis (p. 42). By describing high-rise buildings as disrupting the city's landscape and skyline, GAM acknowledged that high-rise buildings would negatively influence the city's urban fabric. Furthermore, as architect Ayman Zuaiter pointed out, GAM's justification of its regulation for high-rise buildings in wadis showed that this regulation was based on a "formalistic study" that prioritized the skyline of the city over the social aspects of the neighborhoods where high-rise buildings were allowed (personal communication, September 2, 2010). In fact, city officials' rhetoric supported this point. They said that they regulated high-rise buildings in wadis so that they would "control" and "preserve" the "image of the city" (R. Odeh, personal communication, July 15, 2010). But Sanaya's site connected visually and socially with Eastern Amman, with its modest low-rise buildings and working- and lower-middle-class residents, rather than with Western Amman. Thus, it is safe to conclude that high-rise buildings were not regulated in response to market demands, as GAM claimed, as much as they were a means to image Amman as a competitive modern city, hoping the new image would attract investors, tourists, and businesses and consequently create demand for the office, residential, and commercial spaces of these high-rise buildings.

Spectacular developments

Early twenty-first-century megaprojects in Amman were conceived as spectacular modern developments. To create the desired image of these developments and the city, the developers hired regionally and, more important, internationally acclaimed architects. By the late twentieth century, employing the services of highly reputable international architects, or starchitects as they are often called, had become important for creating spectacular high-quality developments that would enhance the image of the city to which they belonged and help market it worldwide. The most quoted example on the significant role starchitects played in city imaging are Frank Gehry's designs for the Guggenheim Museum in Bilbao (completed 1997), which dramatically transformed the image of the city and enhanced its economy. Similarly, the role starchitects, such as Skidmore, Owings & Merrill (SOM) and Rem Koolhaas, played in re-imaging and marketing Dubai (through built and unbuilt designs for the city) in the late twentieth and early twenty-first centuries is undeniable (see Kanna, 2011). In Amman, the developers of Sanaya Amman hired the internationally renowned Murphy/Jahn. Known for their spectacular high-rise buildings in the United States, Western Europe, and the Gulf states, Murphy/Jahn constituted an integral part of the iconicity of Sanaya. Similarly, in The New Downtown developers employed famous architects such as Foster + Partners, Claudio Nardi, and Architecture-Studio for the designs of some buildings in this development. The Abdali advertisements emphasize the role of starchitects in creating this project, speaking of this development's buildings as "designed by some of the world's most celebrated studios" and listing names of architectural and planning firms that they represent as internationally renowned (AID, n.d.b). The names include internationally acclaimed firms, but they include firms that are known only regionally or nationally. The Abdali developers were not concerned with providing the audiences of the advertisements with facts about this development; rather, they wanted to create an image for The New Downtown fit for a global Amman and with potential for great profit through the association of this development with internationally renowned architects.

For the buildings at the IT Sector in The New Downtown, the developers and their starchitects sought a high-tech character, and, thus, glass curtain walls and metal finishes were encouraged on these buildings (AID, n.d.a). AID exempted high-rise buildings in the IT Sector from regulation of building shape, finishing materials, and colors, among other things (AID, n.d.a). Regardless of their location, high-rise buildings in Abdali were considered landmark buildings, and, thus, architects were allowed more room for creativity. Relaxation of regulation for tall buildings also can be seen as a means to attract big developers to invest in Abdali. Still, some developers of high-rise buildings in Abdali were able to dismiss AID's building regulations with regards to façade colors and architectural vocabulary. For example, the developers of Abdali Gateway (Figure 2.6) on the southern side of the Abdali development replaced the yellow color required by AID's regulations with black and white. Similarly, this development's façade composition, which is remarkable for its apparently random pixel pattern, did not match its surroundings and interrupted the continuity of the southern façade of the Abdali development. Just as AID and LACECO wanted an image that distinguished The New Downtown from buildings in the neighborhood, Abdali Gateway developers and architects wanted to distinguish their buildings from their surroundings. The Abdali development's image was compromised in concession to big developers' requirements. It was the same logic of capital that made the implementation of the Abdali development in the heart of Amman possible, compromising the city's skyline and landscape.

Like their counterparts in Abdali, the starchitects of Sanaya prepared a design for this development that was unusual in Amman, a "daring" design as the developers described it ("Limitless digs," 2009; McMeeken, 2009). Sanaya's twin towers, which had simple rectangular floor plans, split away from each other as they rose up, leaving the buildings inclined (see Figure 1.8).[4] The façades of these buildings had a double skin: the internal of glass and the external of a stone mesh. The developers' rhetoric stressed the appearance of these buildings, emphasizing the different colors of the façades during the day and night as the stone mesh would reflect sun rays during the day and allow light from the interior of the buildings to illuminate the façades at night. It is tempting to say that the extensive use of stone on the façades of the Sanaya development, although in a way new to Amman, would have produced Sanaya as a hybrid development that would

Figure 2.6 View of the Abdali Gateway development in The New Downtown.

Note: Taken by May Musa on July 15, 2016.

have connected with the city's landscape and its stone-finished buildings. But, the large scale of this development, particularly its significant height, its unusual form, and the glazed suspended swimming pool as well as the steel-and-glass bridges connecting Sanaya's twin buildings made it unlikely that Sanaya would have blended with its surroundings, particularly the modest low-rise buildings in the neighborhood.

Achieving a satisfactory relation between high-rise buildings and their surroundings was a challenge many architects designing in the city faced in the early twenty-first century. Jordan Gate's architects admitted that it was a great challenge to "create a project of such unusual size for Amman and yet keep it sympathetic to the dominant low rise fabric of the city" (Tukan, n.d., p. 2; see Figures 1.6, 1.7, and 2.5). The Consolidated Consultants-Jafar Tukan Architects designed Jordan Gate so that it would include a low-rise base primarily finished in stone, which would be in harmony with the surrounding low-rise, stone-sheathed urban fabric (Tukan, n.d., p. 2). However, site observation showed that stone used on Jordan Gate was not in harmony with the surrounding buildings. While the surrounding urban fabric had a white color, Jordan Gate's base had a yellow color; and while the surrounding urban fabric had a mixture of textures, Jordan Gate's base had a smooth texture. Both the color and texture of stone used on the façades of this development were similar to those the Abdali developers regulated for buildings in The New Downtown. The architects of Jordan Gate designed a high-rise development in Abdali around the same time they designed Jordan Gate. Possibly, they were influenced by the Abdali regulations in their selection of stone color and texture. As in Abdali, it was likely that the smooth texture of stone on the façades of Jordan Gate's base was selected to emphasize the modern character of this development, and the selection of the yellow color for stone was to differentiate it from the surrounding urban fabric.

If Jordan Gate's base was only partly in harmony with its surroundings, the two high-rise buildings of this development completely disconnected from their urban context. These buildings were finished in glazed curtain walls, which departed from Tukan's use of stone in most of his buildings in the city. In fact, Tukan was well known in Jordan for his mastery of stone in buildings. Architects and architectural historians in the country agreed that Tukan was a pioneer in introducing new textures and details of stone to the country, many of which were adopted by architects and became common in Amman. When asked about whether the decision to use glazed curtain walls on Jordan Gate was made by the architects or by the developers, Tukan asserted that it was his own decision to use glass curtain walls (personal communication, July 15, 2010). Glass curtain walls were rare in Amman, particularly on such tall buildings, but very common in the Gulf.

The fascination with glass and its extensive use on buildings became increasingly common as early as the early twentieth century in Western Europe and the United States. Since Joseph Paxton's Crystal Palace (1851), glass has become associated with modernity and technological innovation, among others. Explaining his design approach to Jordan Gate's buildings, Tukan mentioned that he "conceive[d] them as two minimalistic crystals rising high above the horizon dissolving in the surrounding sky" (Tukan, n.d., p. 2). Tukan mentioned how the glass curtain walls had sloping tops and were designed so that no metal parts were visible on the buildings' façades, emphasizing the lightness and transparency of the buildings (Tukan, n.d., p. 2). The architects' rendering of Jordan Gate conveyed, to some extent, the conception of this development as described by Tukan. Although sometimes from certain angles these buildings look light, to borrow Tukan's word, more often than not they look heavy and disrupted the city's skyline (see Figures 1.1, 1.6, 1.7, and 2.5). Tukan spoke about how glass on the buildings would reflect the skies and change color during day and night, "dramatiz[ing] the mystical presence of such an urban landmark" (Tukan, n.d., p. 2). For some people in the neighborhood and in the surrounding neighborhoods, however, the reflective glass caused annoying glare, which required tenants and property owners to take measures to protect themselves from sun reflection such as installing awnings. The mystical quality of Jordan Gate that Tukan mentioned was absent; and some individuals in the city went so far as to refer to this development as the "ghost." However, people's judgment of Jordan Gate might have been influenced by its look at night because as of this writing the buildings are not completed and stand remarkably tall and unlit.

Regardless of how people viewed Jordan Gate, Tukan's description of this development's conceptual designs showed how significant the image was in the conceptualization of Jordan Gate. The imaging of this development was similar to the imaging of Sanaya, particularly in the emphasis on the surfaces of the buildings and their changing appearance during day and night. Interestingly, both Helmut Jahn, president and CEO of Murphy/Jahn, and Tukan were influenced by the Modern school of architecture, particularly by the work of Mies van der Rohe (Rackwitz, 2011; Tukan, 1999). These architects, however, adapted Modernism differently. Ironically, it was Sanaya's American architects, not Jordan Gate's Jordanian architects, who chose to use stone on the façades of the high-rise buildings of their development. It is tempting to say that the architects were experimenting in materials new to them. This might have been particularly true for Murphy/Jahn, who were mostly known for their steel-and-glass buildings in the United States and Western Europe. But Consolidated Consultants-Jafar Tukan Architects had used glass curtain walls on many of their buildings in Gulf cities, although glass curtain walls were new on their buildings, particularly Tukan's buildings, in Amman. It is also likely that Sanaya's architects believed their use of stone in such a unique way would have distinguished this development from other large-scale developments in Amman as well as in other cities, adding to its symbolic capital, whereas Jordan Gate's architects found symbolic capital in glass as a material associated with innovation and modernity.

Of course, one could not rule out the agency of the developers in the selection of these developments' finishing materials and the creation of their image. Although Jordan Gate's architects said they were responsible for selecting glass curtain walls, they mentioned that the developers provided them with "schematic designs" for these buildings (J. Tukan, personal communication, July 15, 2010). These schematic designs "defined the general idea of the massing," among other things (J. Tukan, personal communication, July 15, 2010). It is likely that such designs showed glazed tall buildings, particularly as they came from Gulf-state developers. Glazed high-rise buildings had been a distinctive marker for the urban built environment in the Gulf in the late twentieth and early twenty-first centuries. Furthermore, the developers of Jordan Gate took pride in this project's finishing material. Al Hamad, for example, said that glass was used to "achieve the architectural and aesthetic goals the project sought" ("(AL Hamad) tunjiz," 2006). In their designs for DAMAC's The Lofts and The Heights at The New Downtown, Consolidated Consultants-Jafar Tukan Architects used stone more extensively on the façades of this development. The agency of AID, the main developers of Abdali, and their planners and architects who set building regulations for this development was evident in shaping DAMAC's and other buildings in the Abdali development. Similarly, the agency of the developers of Sanaya with regard to the use of stone as a finishing material on the façades of this development should not be dismissed. In fact, Limitless emphasized that the company used local building materials in its developments as a part of Limitless's environment-friendly strategies.

The preceding discussion shows that the producers of megaprojects in early twenty-first-century Amman, be they the state, city officials, private developers, architects, or planners, were concerned with image building. They sought for these developments a modern image, which they believed would make the developments competitive at the local, national, regional, and global levels. More important, these megaprojects constituted an integral part of the image that decision-makers sought for the city: an image that would construct Amman as a competitive global city. This image of Amman was to be created through a modern downtown similar to those in other modern cities, spectacular high-rise buildings, modern finishing materials, innovative use of traditional materials, and the city's association with names of starchitects.

The power of corporate developers, particularly Gulf corporations, and the state was dominant in creating this city image. However, corporations competed for power among themselves. City officials exercised power through setting building regulations that could change the city's appearance. They wanted to capture Gulf capital flows and "enhance" the image of the city. This, they believed, would increase the city's competitiveness in the regional and global market and strengthen its economy as well as the country's economy. The agency of the private architects and planners was also operative in shaping the city's megaprojects and consequently the image of the city. However, by commissioning certain architects for the design of their developments, the developers would have already limited the options for the shape of these developments. For example, when AID assigned LACECO for the designs of the Abdali development, they had in mind LACECO's previous work on Beirut Central District. Had AID assigned Rasem Badran, who was known for his tradition-inspired designs, for this job, the image of The New Downtown would likely have been completely different.

In the early twenty-first century, ideas and images transferred to Amman from the Arab Gulf states, the West, and, to a lesser degree in the case of the Abdali development, Lebanon. The result was sometimes developments more similar to those in other places, particularly Gulf cities, than those in Amman, other times hybrid developments. Gulf capital flows made the transfer of ideas and images larger and their adoption and adaptation more likely, and transformed the city's urban built environment. Not only do Amman's contemporary megaprojects create images to see but also they constitute a significant part of the commodified spaces of Amman.

Commodified spaces

In their continuous pursuit of profit, capitalists produce built environments of various scales, even whole cities, as commodified spaces for public consumption (Harvey, 1991; also see Harvey, 1989, 1990). Spectacular buildings, landscapes, and urban spaces are envisioned and then become an integral part of people's daily life and the center of attention. They become a signifier of qualities such as happiness, joyfulness, and eliteness, hiding the processes that produced them that have nothing to do with joy or happiness. Believing that these buildings and spaces can give them the qualities they signify, people begin to compete to occupy or acquire spaces in the spectacular built environments and shop the fetishized commodities displayed in these environments.[5]

In this sense, the built environment becomes a large-scale fetishized commodity, which attests to the dominant role of commodities in modern societies. Thus, developers produce urban developments as a marketable commodity, along with the fetishism, and city officials strive to produce and construct their city as a spectacular place for consumption, hoping to strengthen the city's economy. Megaprojects in early twenty-first-century Amman were a significant example of producing the built environment, and the city, as a commodity for consumption.

The developers of contemporary megaprojects in Amman made sure their developments consisted of commodified spaces both for work and living and, most important, entertainment and shopping spaces. The New Downtown was the most significant example of consumption spaces in the city. Thus, the Central Market Place, also called the Abdali Mall, constituted the core of the Abdali development. The plans for this development showed three main poles: the IT Pole at the western end of this development; the Civic Pole at the eastern end; the Commercial Pole, which consisted of the Abdali Mall, at the center (Figure 2.7). The IT Pole was not the place where IT-related manufacturing or services were accommodated; rather it was the place where IT was consumed in office spaces and hotels as well as in the retail stores located at the bases of these buildings. The Civic Pole originally referred to the Abdali development's cultural component, which was planned for the eastern end of The New Downtown to connect this development to the state institutions next to it on the east. But as this component was abandoned to be replaced with developments that fitted well into the consumption spaces of the Abdali development, later plans for Abdali marked the state institutions, including King Abdullah I Mosque and the Parliament building, as the Civic Pole of the Abdali development. However, these preexisting state institutions were not a part of this development. Thus of the three poles shown on the Abdali plans, the Commercial Pole was the only pole The New Downtown actually included when built.

In other words, the Abdali project was planned around the commercial component, that is, the Abdali Mall. It is not surprising then that this component was located at the intersection of the axes connecting the development's poles and those connecting the northern and southern gates (Figures 2.7 and 2.8). The developers of the Abdali Mall as well as AID were explicit about the centrality of this mall to the Abdali development, stating that it was "situated at the heart of the project" (AID, n.d.a, p. 12). So important was the Abdali Mall for AID that they maintained ownership of it while selling most of the rest of the site as serviced plots to other developers (F. Saifi, personal communication, August 5, 2010).[6] According to its owners, this mall would be "one of the largest and most entertaining components" of the Abdali development and "the largest mall in Jordan" (Kabariti,

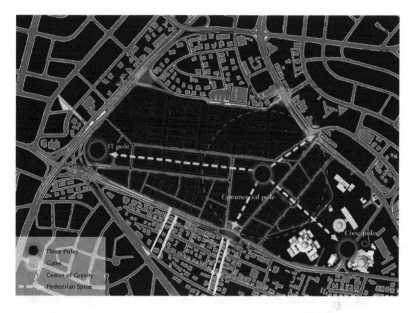

Figure 2.7 Site plan of the Abdali development showing the IT, Commercial, and Civic poles of Phase I of Abdali and the development's gates.

Note: Adapted from *Central Market Place: Book 1: Particular Master Plan Regulations of Sector 4 (Abdali – A New Downtown for Amman, Central Market Place Competition)*, by Abdali Mall Company, 2007, p. 19.

2010). It was "designed in a dynamic modern style," and it would introduce a "new style of living, shopping, [and] dining" so that people would spend "a joyful time" in the Abdali development (Kabariti, 2010).

If the Abdali Mall constituted the "heart" of The New Downtown, the Abdali Boulevard constituted the "spine" of this development. This was a major east-west axis running through Phase I of the Abdali development, connecting the IT Sector in the western end of the Abdali development to the Abdali Mall (see Figure 2.8). In planning the Boulevard, the Abdali planners had in mind "the commercial viability and interest that commercial spines create[d]" (AID, n.d.a, p. 12). Thus, it was designed with retail stores, restaurants, and cafés along its sides, in the lower stories of the office and residential buildings bordering the Boulevard on the sides (AID, n.d.a). Not only was the Boulevard designed as a place for consumption, but it also connected places of consumption together: the mall, the exemplary place of consumption, and the IT Sector, where places of consumption, such as hotels and retail stores placed in their bases as well as in the bases of office buildings, were located. The Boulevard's developers – United Real Estate

Figure 2.8 Site plan of the Abdali development.

Note: Adapted from Abdali Investment and Development's promotional material of Abdali.

Company–Jordan, who are a part of AID joint venture – spoke of its "state-of-the-art" buildings, "exciting" street shops, and "breathtaking" rooftops ("Visualizing the essence," 2009). They viewed it as "the premier entertainment and leisure destination in Amman, inviting visitors to experience a new and vibrant lifestyle, day and night" ("On the rise," 2009). They even went so far as to compare the Boulevard to Paris's Champs-Elysées and London's Oxford Street ("On the rise," 2009), two of the busiest commercial avenues in Europe. The Champs-Elysées is known for its upscale retail stores, restaurants, and cafés as well as for the spectacular parades and other events it hosts. At 70 meters wide, the Champs-Elysées is definitely much more spacious than the Abdali Boulevard at 20 meters, and Paris is certainly more of a world destination than Amman. Still, the comparison made by the Abdali Boulevard's developers was interesting because it showed the ambitions of development corporations investing in Amman in the early twenty-first century, and how urban planning ideas and models integral to capitalist economies and deeply rooted in the West transferred to Amman to reshape its urban built environment. As a commodified urban space, the Boulevard expresses and constructs Debord's (1967/1994) society of the spectacle, a modern consumer society in which images mediate social relations.

The Abdali Mall and Boulevard were not the only shopping and entertainment spaces in The New Downtown. Many developments in this project were required or encouraged to include retail stores at the lower stories (AID, n.d.a; AID, 2006). The stores were required to have galleries and wide shop windows to "encourage transparency and animate streets [and] sidewalks" (AID, n.d.a, p. 48). Even store shutters were to be "transparent" so that "display windows [were] always visible" (p. 37). Designed to attract consumers who have the means to spend, the Abdali upscale stores were unlike the modest stores in downtown Amman, for example, where affordable merchandise was displayed on walkways in front of stores or hung from canopies or galleries' ceilings (see Figure 2.1). Throughout The New Downtown, walkways and piazzas were "enlivened" by upscale cafés and restaurants (AID, n.d.a, p. 12). These were a part of the Abdali regulations and designs that would ensure producing Abdali as a commodity, which visitors would consume as they gaze at commodities displayed there, and at one another.

The Abdali developers wanted to ensure that the "consumerist space" – Sklair's (2010, p. 147) term for the space where "users are encouraged and provided with opportunities to spend money" – was as central for Phase II of the Abdali development as it was for the previous phase. Thus, the plans for Phase II showed a commercial spine, similar to the Abdali Boulevard, running through this development (see Figure 2.8). Somewhere in the center of this spine was a large spherical structure, which included retail stores and entertainment spaces, surrounded by high-rise residential buildings, which included retail stores at their bases (AID, 2009). The planners referred to this part of Phase II of the Abdali development as "the spectacular event" (AID, 2009), which supports the conclusion that The New Downtown was conceived as a commodity for consumption.

As in the Abdali development, shopping and entertainment spaces were conceived as a significant part of Jordan Gate and Sanaya Amman. It is in the upscale retail and entertainment spaces occupying the five-story base of Jordan Gate that fetishized commodities will be displayed, gazed at, bought and sold. These spaces are Jordan Gate's most obvious spaces to serve image building, image consumption, and communication through images. Similarly, designer boutiques and gourmet restaurants and cafés would have occupied the lower stories of the unrealized Sanaya. The glazed façades of these spaces of consumption were meant to connect shopping and entertainment spaces with the plaza outside. Sanaya's plaza would have served not only as a recreation space or a space for socialization and relaxation, as the developers described it, but also, and most important, as an expansion for the realm of the consumerist space. It would have attracted visitors to this development, some of whom would have been overwhelmed by the extensive display of commodities and views of shoppers and diners in Sanaya's stores and restaurants and would have become consumers of these spaces.

Shopping, dining, and entertainment spaces at Amman's early twenty-first-century megaprojects are the most obvious component of the consumerist space in the city, for it is in such places that commodities are displayed and shopping, a significant activity in Amman's modern society, takes place. But in fact all buildings and spaces in these megaprojects were conceived as commodified spaces, of which the image was an integral part. As Sklair (2010) points out, under contemporary globalization, iconic and monumental buildings become significant for the production of the consumerist space. Thus, the new megaprojects in Amman are different from the city's unpretentious, utilitarian buildings that respected the human scale. They also are larger and more spectacular than consumption spaces the city already had. The monumental scale of the Abdali development and its high-tech high-rise buildings and spectacular structures designed by internationally and regionally renowned architects played a role in commodifying Abdali's spaces. Hotel buildings also are an important part of the Abdali development's consumerist space, designed to be among the tallest buildings in this development as well as in Amman, located on sites that had the highest elevation for high visibility, and finished in innovative materials (AID, n.d.a). Residential developments in The New Downtown, such as The Lofts and The Heights, are not only spaces for living but also for consumption as they include, in addition to retail stores, entertainment spaces, fitness clubs, swimming pools, and supporting facilities. Similarly, the two high-rise buildings of Jordan Gate were a significant part of this development's spaces of consumption. Produced to project a modern image that will attract visitors and consumers, they were located at a prominent site that insured high visibility; they were designed to surpass the tallest building in Amman; they were finished in glass, a material associated with transparency and vision, display and the gaze, among others. Likewise, Sanaya's iconicity, record-breaking height, unusual inclined structure, and glazed skybridges and swimming pool were conceived as an integral part of this development's consumerist space. Sanaya's luxurious apartments, lofts, and penthouses as well as its leisure amenities would have served an upscale lifestyle based on commodity consumption and the significance of the image – a lifestyle in which upmarket commodities are consumed for the qualities they signify and for the image they project. More important, these spaces, like their counterparts at Abdali and Jordan Gate, would have contributed to the construction of such a lifestyle as the new normal style of living.

The developers of Amman's megaprojects made sure that the city and its natural landscape became a commodity that would earn them profit. This can be inferred from the emphasis on the views from these developments. Thus unlike ordinary rooftops in Amman, where water tanks, satellite dishes, and clotheslines are placed, spectacular rooftops at The New Downtown are used as terraces, gardens, and swimming pools ("Ihalat 'ata' Boulevard," 2007) from where the Abdali development and the city at large can be experienced. The developers of Sanaya Amman also were concerned with the views of the city from this development, and they spoke proudly of the stunning views that Sanaya's buildings will allow (Limitless, n.d.). However, the surroundings of Sanaya had low-income neighborhoods, which were not the kind of view one would expect from an upscale development such as Sanaya; there was no river, sea, or forest to look at. But the image from Sanaya, particularly from the upper section, would not have showed details of the context. That Sanaya's surroundings would have looked small and abstract from the top would have been a view worthy of looking at for many who belonged to the modern culture in which the image ruled. Furthermore, Amman's hilly landscape and its skyline were an important part of the city image promoted by the Sanaya developers, an irony because the city's landscape and skyline were being damaged by the very development that imaged them.

How do the public in Amman view and interact with the new megaprojects, and who are the consumers of these developments and participants in their spectacular events? The New Downtown, Jordan Gate, and Sanaya Amman produced images and spaces that city residents, visitors, and business persons, seeking prestige, distinction, happiness, or other qualities associated with these spectacular developments, will compete to consume. In addition, these developments and the developers' discourses on them help create a lifestyle of consumption. Comments by individuals interviewed over the course of this research showed that the public in the city understood Jordan Gate, even before it was completed, as a spectacular space of consumption. Adil, a middle-class young man, said that he liked this development because it was a "beautiful view," which "enhanced the shape of the neighborhood" (personal communication, September 29, 2010). He added that although this was an upscale development and the office and hotel buildings would be accessible only to those people who had business there, everyone would be able to visit the mall and the entertainment spaces in Jordan Gate. Ahmed, a middle-class young man, believed that designer stores in the mall were a big advantage of Jordan Gate as they would introduce the latest fashion trends and the right way to don such trends (personal communication, September 30, 2010). Atif, a middle-aged small business owner, liked the mall in this development most and said, "I will shop there instead of shopping at more distant malls" (personal communication, September 28, 2010). Sherif said that Jordan Gate had a "distinctive shape" and

it transformed the neighborhood into a more "dynamic," "joyful," "prestigious" place (personal communication, September 30, 2010). He added,
however, that as someone of a limited income, he only could gaze at this
development from afar and would not enjoy being among the restaurants,
hotel, and shops.

With these disparities, Jordan Gate will likely widen class difference.
The most telling example of how megaprojects such as this development
contribute to the intensification of social polarization were the comments
made by Mohammad who viewed Jordan Gate as "a beautiful landmark"
that helped him find his way in the city (personal communication, October 4, 2010). He wished it included affordable housing for young men like
him, but believed that "not everyone could interact with this development."
Working-class people, according to Mohammad, would not even visit the
mall or cafés in this development. Not only did he attribute this to the lack
of material resources for these people, but also believed that low-income
people would be intimidated by commodities sold in this development.
Mohammad said, "working-class people will not know the kind of meals
served in Jordan Gate's upscale restaurants and cafés." Humble people from
his class, Mohammad added, would visit less sophisticated places, "places
commensurate with their understanding and their limited resources." In contrast, "developed" upper-class people, Mohammad said, "have the money
to spend in Jordan Gate as well as the culture and understanding needed to
interact with this development's mall, restaurants, and health club."

Like Jordan Gate, The New Downtown might not have been as inviting
to working-class people as it was for the upper-class segment of Amman's
residents, tourists, and business persons, despite the rhetoric of the Abdali
developers that indicated otherwise. The developers and their planners
and architects confirmed that Abdali was not a gated community (R. Abou
Rayan, personal communication, August 2 and 8, 2010). The development
is not surrounded by walls, and the "gates" shown on the Abdali plans do not
control access to this development; rather, they only visually define entry
points to The New Downtown and help orient people in space (R. Abou
Rayan, personal communication, August 2 and 8, 2010). According to the
developers, access to residential and office spaces is limited to those who
live, work, or have business there. However, spaces such as the Abdali Mall,
the Boulevard, restaurants, and cafés, which are major sites of consumption,
are open to people from all walks of life. This makes sense, as it is in the
interest of the developers to draw as many people as possible to Abdali in
order to increase consumption and encourage a lifestyle of consumption.

Still, The New Downtown will likely increase social polarization in the
city, which scholars and other individuals in the city recognized. For example, Andrew was critical of corporations redefining the city spaces in order to

market the city and serve their own interest (personal communication, January 17, 2010). For him, the rich in the city might have decided to consider Abdali the downtown, but this development was by no means the downtown for the poor. Similarly, Nahhas (2015) found that the average-income city resident could not afford dining or shopping at The New Downtown, which served more the upper class in the city. Leena also was aware that although the Abdali development would serve some functions of the downtown, mainly providing main offices for big businesses, it would not be the same as the old downtown (personal communication, October 3, 2010). She mentioned that popular street vendors would not be a part of the Abdali development and its everyday experience. Leena, therefore, thought the developers should not have named this development the downtown. Likewise, a blogger urged the city residents not to refer to the Abdali project as the downtown, because this project could not compare to Amman's historic downtown and referring to it as the downtown was only in the interest of the foreign developers (Al-Assi, 2014). Daher (2007, p. 276) was also critical of the name of this development, which he viewed as an indication of a "symbolic replacement of the existing historic downtown." The name "Abdali, The Central Business District of Amman," which the developers came up with for their project in 2010, can be understood, at least in part, in relation to this criticism and resistance to the developers' designation of the Abdali development as the new downtown of Amman. But referring to this development as the new downtown was never abolished (see AID, 2015), for the developers and state needed to establish this development as the downtown of Amman, the downtown that, according to AID (n.d.b), would "transform the capital into one of the most advanced hubs in the world."

The Abdali development was insensitive to the complex urban life as experienced by many people in the neighborhood and the city. The designs of this development separated it from its surroundings and defined it as the modern, joyful, clean environment. The ring road around the Abdali site isolated this development from the environment outside (AID, n.d.a). The yellow smoothly finished stone on its buildings was meant to differentiate the "modern" Abdali development from the "rural" character of stone on neighboring buildings (AID, n.d.a, p. 49). Trees were thought of as a "fence" to separate the Abdali development from the outside, to "isolate the site from neighboring buildings where activity [was] dense and form[ed] a certain congestion and noise pollution," and to "minimize . . . discomfort" (AID, n.d.a, p. 19). Moreover, the neighborhood of the Abdali was cleansed of the busy Abdali transport hub and facilities such as street vendors and Friday Market – a weekly outdoor market held on Fridays that had attracted many city residents shopping for affordable foods and clothes and had sustained the livelihood of many vendors and their families. For decades, these had served Amman's residents, particularly the working-class segment, but these spaces were squeezed out because they no longer matched the modern image and upscale consumption that The New Downtown created.[7] These arrangements, among others, defined Abdali as an exclusive development. Thus a scholar such as Daher (2007, p. 276) referred to the Abdali development as an "elitist urban island."

Some city residents began to accept the new standards of living that the city's contemporary megaprojects construct. Even someone who talked about how the Abdali development encouraged landlords in the neighborhood to raise the rents on tenants or redevelop their properties, pushing her home-based tailor, as well as others, to move out of her place and lose customers, felt the urge to visit Abdali and shop in its fancy spaces before they opened to the public (personal communication, October 19, 2010). Years later, a visitor to the Abdali Mall would praise the beautiful spaces of this mall and the large areas dedicated to designer brands that, unlike smaller areas in other malls, would allow the display of full designer collections (Sadeq, 2016). Other visitors were so excited about the mall, particularly its looks and wide variety of merchandise and international brand names, and they mentioned that they would visit this mall and shop there often ("Al-Ara'," 2016). Similarly, while many people interviewed for my research talked about Sanaya's unsuitability for the city, that it was insensitive to the difficult economic situation of the majority of the population in Amman, and that it was designed for the upper-class segment of the society and wealthy people from outside Jordan, even those who criticized Sanaya wished they could be a part of the lifestyle suggested by this development. There were others who, without the means to own a place in Sanaya, were not critical of this development and would have liked to be a part of it. For example, commenting on a blog post wondering who the prospective buyers of the upscale apartments in Sanaya were, a blogger wrote, "I would definitely buy one if [I] had the money and it had a balcony" ("Would you buy," 2008). Another responded, "I would buy one. Nice pool!" ("Would you buy," 2008).

The pool was ostentatious and contentious. Regardless of how much the developers talked about water-conserving measures they adopted in the designs of Sanaya Amman, the pool would have reminded people in the water-scarce city of how resources were unfairly distributed. Comments made by individuals I interviewed and bloggers support this conclusion (see "Would you buy," 2008). Furthermore, the "display" of people swimming and sun bathing in Sanaya's pool would have intensified social polarization in the city and the country in which, according to Arnold (2008), 50 percent of the population were unable to own a house of 65 square meters or smaller. Some individuals were critical of Sanaya's swimming pool and recreation spaces as well as its luxury apartments, pointing out that many in the city could not even afford food due to the increasingly rising food prices (personal communications, October 2010). Kareem said, "really! A suspended glazed swimming pool in Amman! What were city officials thinking when they approved this development?" (personal communication, October 18, 2010). City officials wanted to project Amman as a modern city, capitalizing on Gulf capital. They wanted to market the city as a perfect place for living and entertainment for those who can afford an upscale lifestyle and who were a part of the society of the spectacle. City officials were a powerful agent not only in conceiving Sanaya, and other commodified developments in Amman, but also in shaping the city residents into a consumer society in which social life was mediated by images.

In the early twenty-first century, Amman's urban built environment was being produced, experienced, and constructed as a commodified environment, which was integral to capitalist means of production. Amman's megaprojects produced spectacular, theatrical spaces for display and consumption, which were unprecedented in the city. They produced upscale consumerist spaces, which became a model to emulate, engendering similar developments in Amman. They promoted a lifestyle in which the fetishized commodity ruled and helped present the city residents as and shape them into a society of the spectacle. But Amman's spaces of consumption are not entirely alien from the city's society. City residents have been transforming into a consumer society since the late twentieth century. This transformation was influenced by globalization processes, including the flows of capital, people, ideologies, ideas, and images. The Gulf states had a strong influence on producing the commodified spaces of Amman. But these states did not invent such spaces; they were influenced by Western ideas, images, and consumption patterns dictated by capitalists' interests. In Amman, state and city officials were a powerful agent in the commodification of the city. State and city officials wanted to capture capital flows from the Gulf and produce developments similar to those in modern cities, which would attract more capital, transnational businesses, and tourists and would place Amman on what they believed the right track to globality. Thus, early twenty-first-century megaprojects in Amman, as in Dubai and many other places, were not produced in response to the needs of the majority of the city residents: working- and middle-class people. In fact, they intensified social inequality in the city. However, the producers of megaprojects knew that even working- and middle-class segments of the society could help make these developments a success. Although the public did not participate in the decision to produce the city's megaprojects as a commodity, they were an agent in the production of these spaces, not least through their adoption of a lifestyle based on the image and the commodity, a lifestyle that encouraged the commodification of the built environment and served corporations. These corporations could then manipulate images and commodities and set new standards for what "the" lifestyle should look like, continuously shaping and reshaping the city residents into a society of the spectacle.

Notes

1 In 2010, some Abdali plans on the wall of LACECO offices at the Abdali site showed the Abdali cultural component, as well as the university sector. LACECO's R. Abou Rayan pointed out that these were old plans dating back to the Abdali project's early phase and they had been changed, but she did not know when (personal communication, August 2 and 8, 2010). A 2006 Abdali document referred to the project's cultural component, as well as the university sector (see AID, 2006, p. 26). Later documents did not make any reference to these parts of the Abdali project (see Abdali Mall Company [AMC], 2007).
2 Throughout this book, I use pseudonyms for the interviewees from the public to protect the privacy of the research participants.
3 For example, see emphasis put on tourism in Greater Amman Municipality's news item on the painting of the façades of old buildings in the downtown (Greater Amman Municipality [GAM], 2008b).
4 According to architect R. Dahdaleh of Consolidated Consultants-Jafar Tukan Architects, the local coordinators and supervising engineers for Sanaya Amman, these buildings were designed with some nine meters' difference between the outer face of the building at the bottom and top (personal communication, July 2010).
5 Studying the fetishism of commodities is an essential part of Karl Marx's project on capitalism. By uncovering fetishism, Marx sought to unveil the dynamics of capitalism. Describing Marx's conceptualization of commodity fetishism, Harvey (1991, p. 52) writes, "Commodities . . . are produced through social labor and come to us through a process of market exchange . . . [which] obscures the myriad social relations that enter into commodity production, transport, and marketing." For more information on Marx's work on commodity fetishism, see Marx (1967, 1973).
6 The Abdali Mall Company is the owner of the Abdali Mall. This company, however, consists of Abdali Investment and Development (AID) and United Real Estate Company-Jordan, one of the companies in the AID joint venture (AID, 2015).
7 For more on Greater Amman Municipality's decision to move the Friday Market from Abdali, see Freij (2014) and Cozzens (2014). For the controversy surrounding this decision and vendors' initial resistance to move out, see Cozzens (2014).

References

Abdali Investment and Development (AID). (n.d.a). *Abdali – A New Downtown for Amman: Sector regulations brief, Sector 1: IT Sector.*
Abdali Investment and Development (AID). (n.d.b). Abdali Downtown: The New Downtown of Amman – A modern landmark in the making [Advertorial; obtained from AID].
Abdali Investment and Development (AID). (2006). *Abdali – A New Downtown for Amman: Development brief – Sector 5E.*

Abdali Investment and Development (AID). (2009). *Abdali master plan extension (phase 2 & 3): The Urban Park, Civil Defense presentation.*

Abdali Investment and Development (AID). (2010). Abdali, the Central Business District of Amman [obtained from AID].

Abdali Investment and Development (AID). (2015). The New Downtown of Amman. Retrieved March 26, 2016, from http://www.abdali.jo/pdf/abdali-2015.pdf.

Abdali Mall Company (AMC). (2007). *Central Market Place: Book 1: Particular master plan regulations of Sector 4 (Abdali – A New Downtown for Amman, Central Market Place competition).*

Abdali PSC launches new campaign. (2008). *Abdali Newsletter, 5,* 5.

"Abu-Ghazaleh" tarfud bay 'mabaniha wa 'aqaratiha fi al-'Abdali ["Abu-Ghazaleh" refuses to sell its buildings and real estate properties at Abdali; in Arabic]. (2006, December 13). *Alghad.*

Al-Ara' [Views; in Arabic]. (2016). Abdali Mall Facebook. Retrieved August 4, 2016, from https://www.facebook.com/AbdaliMall/reviews?ref=page_internal.

Al-Asad, M. (2007, March 1). The Dubai model. *The Jordan Times.* Retrieved August 13, 2016, from http://www.csbe.org/publications-and-resources/urban-crossroads/the-dubai-model/.

Al-Asad, M. (2008, September 11). Amman's heart and soul: The downtown area. *The Jordan Times.* Retrieved August 11, 2016, from http://www.csbe.org/publications-and-resources/urban-crossroads/amman-s-heart-and-soul-the-downtown-area/.

Al-Asad, M. (2012). *Contemporary architecture and urbanism in the Middle East.* Gainesville: University Press of Florida.

Al-Assi, R. (2014, June 12). Stop yourself from referring to the Abdali project as "downtown". It is not downtown. *AndFarAway.* Retrieved August 1, 2016, from http://www.andfaraway.net/blog/2014/06/12/stop-yourself-from-referring-to-the-abdali-project-as-downtown-it-is-not-downtown/.

Arnold, T. (2008, September 19). Jordan's growing pains. *Arabian Business.com.* Retrieved August 14, 2016, from http://www.arabianbusiness.com/jordan-s-growing-pains-43090.html.

Bayan Holding, Gulf Finance House, & Kuwait Finance and Investment Company. (2007, September). Jordan's highest landmark [Advertisement]. *Jordan Property,* inside back cover.

Bayan Holding, Gulf Finance House, & Kuwait Finance and Investment Company. (2007–2008, December–January). [Advertisement on Jordan Gate; in Arabic]. *Jordan Land Magazine,* inside front cover-1.

Cozzens, R. (2014, November 26). What is behind the Abdali Market move? Retrieved August 4, 2016, from http://7iber.com/2014/11/what-is-behind-the-abdali-market-move/#.V6Og4eTqU-1.

Cuadra, M. (2007). The power of images. In M. Al-Asad & M. Musa (Eds.), *Architectural criticism and journalism: Global perspective.* (pp. 75–80). Turin: Umberto Allemandi and Geneva: The Aga Khan Trust for Culture.

Daher, R. (2007). Tourism, heritage, and urban transformations in Jordan and Lebanon: Emerging actors and global-local juxtapositions. In R. Daher (Ed.), *Tourism in the Middle East: Continuity, change, and transformation* (pp. 263–307). Clevedon: Channel View.

Debord, G. (1967/1994). *The society of the spectacle* (D. Nicholson-Smith, Trans.). New York: Zone Books.

Dovey, K. (1999). *Framing places: Mediating power in built form*. London and New York: Routledge.

Dwairi, M. (2005, June 22). Tawqi' ittifaqiyyat bi al-ahruf al-ula li bay' aradi istithmariyya dimn mashru'"al-'Abdali" [Signing with initials contracts for selling investment land within the Abdali project; in Arabic]. *Al Rai*. Retrieved August 11, 2016, from http://www.alrai.com/article/110176.html.

Freij, M. (2014, September 15). Abdali Friday Market to open in new location on Oct. 9 – GAM. Retrieved August 4, 2016, from http://www.jordantimes.com/news/local/abdali-friday-market-open-new-location-oct-9-%E2%80%94-gam.

GFH's Jordan Gate project due for completion early 2011. (2010). Retrieved August 11, 2016, from http://www.zawya.com/mena/en/story/ZAWYA20100905073805/.

Greater Amman Municipality (GAM). (2007). *Interim growth strategy: High density mixed use development manual* [CD]. Amman: Greater Amman Municipality.

Greater Amman Municipality (GAM). (2008a). *The Amman Plan: Metropolitan growth summary report* [CD]. Amman: Greater Amman Municipality.

Greater Amman Municipality (GAM). (2008b, August 27). GAM continues panting [*sic*] project for downtown Amman. Retrieved August 4, 2016, from http://www.ammancity.gov.jo/en/resource/snews.asp?id=FE09EB04-71CC-4AF3-978F-2E2E89A41DBE.

Green, innovative and sustainable projects mark the success story of Limitless. (2009, April–May). *Real Estate & Investment: Middle East*, 28–30.

(Al Hamad) tunjiz qawa'id al-hadid li (Bawwabat al-Urdun) al-usbu' al-muqbil wa (al-Amana) ta'tamid tasamimaha al-mi'mariyya [Al Hamad will complete Jordan Gate's steel foundation next week and the municipality approves its architectural designs; in Arabic]. (2006, February 23). *Al Rai*.

Harvey, D. (1989). *The urban experience*. Baltimore: Johns Hopkins University Press.

Harvey, D. (1990). *The condition of postmodernity: An enquiry into the origins of cultural change*. New York: Blackwell.

Harvey, D. (1991). The urban face of capitalism. In J. F. Hart (Ed.), *Our changing cities* (pp. 51–66). Baltimore and London: Johns Hopkins University Press.

Harvey, D. (2001a). The art of rent: Globalization and the commodification of culture. In *Spaces of capital: Towards a critical geography* (pp. 394–411). New York: Routledge.

Harvey, D. (2001b). A view from Federal Hill. In *Spaces of capital: Towards a critical geography* (pp. 128–157). New York: Routledge.

Harvey, D. (2005). *The new imperialism*. Oxford: Oxford University Press.

Hazaimeh, H. (2007, August 28). Jordan Gate stands as tallest building in town. *The Jordan Times*, p. 1.

Ihalat 'ata' Boulevard al-'Abdali 'ala Saudi Oger bi kulfat 300 million dinaran [Awarding the bid for the Abdali Boulevard to Saudi Oger in the amount of 300 million dinars; in Arabic]. (2007, September 9). *Al Rai*. Retrieved August 14, 2016, from http://alrai.com/article/238694.html.

Ittifaqiyyat bay' husat al-Amana fi "Bawwabat al-Urdun" tuwaqqa' . . . al-yawm [Agreement to sell shares of the Greater Amman Municipality in "Jordan Gate" to be signed . . . today; in Arabic]. (2007, January 8). *Al Rai*.

Janahi: 40% al-injaz fi mashru' Bawwabat al-Urdun [Janahi: 40% of the Jordan Gate project is completed; in Arabic]. (2007, December 11). *Al Rai*.

Jordan Gate breaks ground: King inaugurates 1st phase of $1 billion Royal Metropolis plan. (2005, May 30). *The Jordan Times*. Retrieved August 11, 2016, from http://www.skyscraperlife.com/jordan/237-project-amman-jordan-gate-towers.html.

Jordan Gate Company. (n.d.). Introducing Jordan Gate [Brochure].

Kabariti, A. (2010). Abdali Mall Company announces the launch of construction at the Central Market Place project. *Abdali Newsletter, 10*, 8.

Kanna, A. (2011). *Dubai: The city as corporation*. Minneapolis: University of Minnesota Press.

Kayyali, A.-W. (2008, April). In the name of the people: A lesson in expropriation. *Venture Magazine*.

Limitless. (n.d.). Sanaya Amman [Brochure].

Limitless digs deep to reach new heights in Jordan. (2009, March 2). Retrieved August 10, 2016, from http://limitless.com/en-gb/newsroom/02-03-2009/Limitless digs deep to reach new heights in Jordan.aspx.

Limitless: Sanaya Amman. (n.d.). Retrieved August 12, 2016, from http://www.limitless.com/en-GB/Projects/Middle East/Sanaya Amman.aspx.

Lynch, K. (1960). *The image of the city*. Boston: MIT Press.

Maani, O. (2007). *High rise towers: An integral part of Amman's urban landscape* [presentation]. Retrieved August 13, 2016, from https://www.scribd.com/doc/505010/Amman-Master-Plan.

Majmu'at Abu-Ghazaleh tuwajjih indaran 'adliyyan li Amanat 'Amman [Abu-Ghazaleh Organization Sues Greater Amman Municipality; in Arabic]. (2007, March 1). *Alghad*.

Makdisi, S. (1997). Laying claim to Beirut: Urban narrative and spatial identity in the age of Solidere. *Critical Inquiry, 23*(3), 660–705.

Malkawi, S., & Kaddoura, H. (2007). *Ontology of Amman: Soul and body – study of the development of the Arab modern city* [in Arabic with a few sections translated into English]. Amman: Nara.

Mallgrave, H.F. (2005). *Modern architectural theory: A historical survey, 1673–1968*. New York: Cambridge University Press.

Marx, K. (1967). *Capital (Volume 1)*. New York: International.

Marx, K. (1973). *Grundrisse*. Harmondsworth, Middlesex: Penguin Books.

Mayor Omar Maani comments on 360°east regarding the Sanaya Amman skyscraper ads. (2009, October 8). *360°east*. Retrieved August 13, 2016, from http://www.360east.com/?p=1136.

McMeeken, R. (2009). Jordan green tower excavations near completion. Retrieved August 13, 2016, from http://www.building.co.uk/news/jordan-green-tower-excavations-near-completion/3135097.article.

Mumtaz, B. (2006, July 13). Desperately seeking Amman. Retrieved August 11, 2016, from http://www.csbe.org/publications-and-resources/urban-crossroads/desperately-seeking-amman/.

Nahhas, R. (2015, October 16). Amman: A city with two downtowns. *Arab Weekly, 27*, p. 24.

On the rise: Abdali Boulevard. (2009). *Abdali Newsletter, 8*, 8.

Rackwitz, J. (2011, November 25). Murphy Jahn Architects. *Mapolis.* Retrieved August 14, 2016, from http://architecture.mapolismagazin.com/content/murphy-jahn-architects.

Sadeq, R. (2016). Retrieved August 4, 2016, from http://m.jeeran.com/amman/abdali-mall-amman.

Saliba, R. (2007). Deconstructing Beirut's reconstruction: 1990–2000 – Coming to terms with the colonial heritage. In M. Al-Asad & M. Musa (Eds.), *Exploring the built environment: Essays on the presentations of Diwan al-Mimar and affiliated public lectures* (pp. 159–172). Amman: Center for the Study of the Built Environment (CSBE) and Darat al Funun – the Khalid Shoman Foundation.

Shamma, M. (2010, February). Al-Mukhattat al-Shumuli: Tumuh yaqfiz 'an al-bu'd al-insani ahyanan [The master plan: An ambition that sometimes bypasses the human aspect; in Arabic]. *Al-Sijill, 8,* 36–38.

Sklair, L. (2010). Iconic architecture and the culture-ideology of consumerism. *Theory, Culture & Society, 27*(5), 135–159.

Summerson, J. (1963). *Classical language of architecture.* London: Methuen.

This insane skyscraper ad abuses Amman! (2009, April 15). *360°east.* Retrieved August 13, 2016, from http://www.360east.com/?p=1129.

$300m Limitless towers set to dwarf Jordan's tallest buildings. (2008, February 14). *Gulf News.* Retrieved August 12, 2016, from http://gulfnews.com/business/property/300m-limitless-towers-set-to-dwarf-jordan-s-tallest-buildings-1.84637.

Tukan, J. (n.d.). Amman Jordan Gate: Why and how?? [Article obtained from J. Tukan on July 15, 2010].

Tukan, J. (1999). Al-Asala wa al-mu'asara – Tajruba shakhssiyya [Genuineness and contemporariness – A personal experience; in Arabic]. *Alam al-Bina, 207,* 15–17.

United Nations – Economic and Social Commission for Western Asia. (2005). *Urbanization and the changing character of the Arab city* (Report No. E/ESCWA/SDD/2005/1). New York: United Nations.

Visualizing the essence of the Boulevard of the new Abdali downtown. (2009). *Abdali Newsletter, 9,* 12.

Wad' hajar asas mashru' Bawwabat al-Urdun . . . al-yawm [Laying the cornerstone for the Jordan Gate project . . . today; in Arabic]. (2005, May 29). *Al Rai.*

Al-Wazani, K. (2006, October 01). Bawwabat al-Urdun: Unju Sa'd! [Jordan Gate: Run for your life Sa'd!; in Arabic]. *Al Rai.*

Would you buy a flat in Amman's newest 300 million dollar tower? (2008, February 16). *360°east.* Retrieved August 14, 2016, from http://www.360east.com/?p=931.

3 Negotiating identity in contemporary megaprojects

The urban built environment plays a significant role in communicating and shaping national, group, and individual identities (see Çinar, 2007; Harvey, 1989, 1990, 1991; King, 1996). Early twenty-first-century megaprojects in Amman strongly related to the question of city residents' identity. An investigation of some of these megaprojects reveals what identities they expressed, created, or expressed and created, what identities they disconnected from, and how and why they did so. This investigation also shows how identity construction through and expression in Amman's built environment related to Gulf capital flows to the city, to the state, to the capitalist system of production, and to power relations in the city. Any study of the relation between the new megaprojects in Amman and the condition that created them, on the one hand, and identity, on the other, cannot be disassociated from the investigation of the nature of the Jordanian identity, particularly the official national identity, because the state was a major player in the production of these megaprojects.

Anderson's (2006) notion of the constructedness of identity applies to identity in Jordan. Official Jordanian national identity is a construct, not an essential thing that has always been there or will always be there in the same form. Like collective identities in other places, national identity in Jordan is hybrid, created through encounters with others. This identity is constantly evolving, continuously shaped and reshaped with the changing economic, political, and sociocultural circumstances in the country (see Frisch, 2002; Massad, 2001; Nasser, 2004). Furthermore, like other national identities, the Jordanian national identity is constructed through sameness and difference: the inclusion of those similar (Jordanians) and the exclusion of the others (see Massad, 2001; Nasser, 2004). The self and the other change in the process of identity reconstruction.[1] Moreover, national identity in Jordan, as in other postcolonial nation-states, includes colonial influences. As Massad (2001) argues, the Jordanian national identity can be understood as a product and an effect of colonial institutions. Not only was the state established and its boundaries delineated by the British colonial power, but also many of the postcolonial state institutions responsible for the construction of the national identity, such as the military and law institutions, followed the colonial model and adopted colonial cultural products, which are "modern inventions dressed up in traditional garb" (p. 7). The postcolonial nation-state disseminated such modern inventions as essentially Jordanian through different state institutions and media discourses.

Rashid Khalidi's argument that national identity in the Arab countries is "not unidimensional" but it involves "multiple identification" (Nasser, 2004, p. 224) applies to national identity in Jordan (Nasser, 2004). But what are the elements that contribute to the multiple nature of national identity in Jordan? How and why are these elements ranked in importance? These are important questions for an analysis of the urban built environment in Amman and the various meanings this environment expresses or constructs. State institutions construct Jordan's official national identity with reference to four elements: diverse population (the tribes versus the others), Islam, Arabs, and modernization and economic development. The emphasis put on one or the other of these elements differs in the official discourse on national identity at different moments of Jordan's history. Frisch (2002) argues that even at a particular moment, official discourse on Jordanian national identity is intentionally ambiguous so that the identity of Jordan can be "shaped and reshaped for instrumental purposes" (p. 89). For Frisch, the fuzzy official discourse on national identity in Jordan is connected to the issue of national and regional security, mainly the heterogeneous population and the vulnerability of the state in the "regional system" (p. 101).

The tribal Jordanian

The population in Jordan, particularly in Amman, is highly diverse, including Syrian and Iraqi refugees, Southeast Asian and Egyptian workers, and other Arab and Western expatriates (Department of Statistics, 2016). What concerns us most here is the diverse population of the Jordanian nationals, which is among the main characteristics of the state and an important element in the construction of Jordanianness. As Massad (2001) points out, the majority of Jordanians have their origins outside the area that became the nation-state of Transjordan in 1921. The 1928 Nationality Law constructed the diverse population living in the then recently established Transjordan state, such as the tribal people of Transjordan, Circassians, Palestinians, Syrians, and Lebanese, as Transjordanians. These people had never identified themselves as such before the establishment of this law. The definition of Jordanianness changed after the 1948 Arab-Israeli War, when the

Palestinian refugees in the country were naturalized, and the West Bank was annexed to Jordan and its Palestinian populations became Jordanian nationals (Massad, 2001).[2] When the West Bank was lost to Israel in 1967, many Palestinian-Jordanians moved to Jordan, particularly Amman, thus outnumbering other ethnic groups in the country. Although Palestinian-Jordanians are just one other among many others in Jordan, they have been of particular concern to the question of national identity in Jordan since the end of 1948. This matter has been pointed out at different times of Jordan's history by many scholars (see Nasser, 2004; Nevo, 2003; Al Oudat & Alshboul, 2010). Al Oudat and Alshboul even argue that the new waves of Palestinians helped create a sense of national identity in Jordan. The overwhelming Palestinian population in Jordan, particularly during the third quarter of the twentieth century, made Transjordanian-Jordanians, or "Real" or "True" Jordanians as tribal Transjordanian-Jordanians came to call themselves and, often, other Transjordanian-Jordanians from non-Palestinian origin, feel threatened by the possibility of being dominated by the Palestinian majority.[3]

Jordan's tribal population constitutes a significant element in the construction of the Jordanian identity (see Massad, 2001; Nevo, 2003; Al Oudat & Alshboul, 2010). Tribesmen (and more recently tribeswomen) have been a significant part of the military institution since the establishment of this institution in Jordan in the late 1920s under the British Mandate.[4] As in many states, the military in Jordan is one of the most important institutions that construct national identity. It is the institution that is established to defend the nation-state, and its flag, anthem, and sense of cohesion are all highly charged with nationalism (Alon, 2007; Massad, 2001). The fact that tribesmen constituted, and still constitute, a great majority in the military played a crucial role in the Bedouinization of Jordan's national identity and culture (Massad, 2001; Susser, 2000). As a result, in the popular imagination, the Jordanian subject became identifiable as "the" Bedouin or tribesperson, and "the" Bedouin or tribal culture became representative of the Jordanian culture. The military – together with other colonial institutions in Jordan – repressed a range of existing cultural material and practices and produced others, many of which were associated with Bedouin culture, as traditional national material and practices (Massad, 2001). In other words, this is an example of what Hobsbawm (1983, p. 2) calls "the invention of tradition": institutions of the postcolonial state adopted the colonial cultural products as the traditional Jordanian products, and nationalists viewed these products as essential (Massad, 2001). However, the Bedouin subject that the colonial state produced, and the postcolonial state takes as its national subject, is not the same Bedouin who preceded the establishment of modern Jordan. The kind of Bedouinism that the state constructs and promotes is a homogenized Bedouin identity and culture, which in reality does not exist (see Al Oudat & Alshboul, 2010). Although tribespeople today define themselves as opposed to non-Bedouin others, particularly the Palestinian other, they are aware of their place within a specific tribe and lineage that excludes other tribes.

How did early twenty-first-century megaprojects in Amman connect with the tribal identity of Jordanians? The formal composition and architectural vocabularies of the study cases did not show any strong connection with the tribal Jordanian. Similarly, notwithstanding a cultural event such as the one that has recently taken place in the open spaces of The New Downtown (Abdali) and staged Jordan's Bedouin heritage, the functions of the new megaprojects did not particularly relate to the tribal Jordanian.[5] Still, tribal identity, as well as otherness, should not be dismissed as irrelevant to the argument of identity as it relates to the new megaprojects in the city. Amman's diverse population, particularly tribespeople as the quintessential Transjordanian-Jordanians and the Palestinian-Jordanians as the quintessential other, constituted a significant part of the production process of the megaprojects and people's perception of these projects. The New Downtown is a telling example of the relation between these megaprojects and identity as it relates to the diverse population in the city. On the one hand, Mawared, a corporation owned by the Jordanian military, is a partner in the Abdali Investment and Development (AID) joint venture developing the Abdali project. Mawared's income from this development will be invested in military-related developments and facilities and in the pension fund of the military, which mostly consists of tribal Jordanians (Mernin, 2007; Parker, 2009). On the other hand, The New Downtown involved the relocation of military buildings, as well as other state buildings, to less central locations and the selling of military- and state-owned land to the private sector. This reflected, at least in part, the diminishing role of state institutions, and consequently deemphasized the status of tribespeople as the major part of the state.

In the early twenty-first century, Amman had a majority of Palestinian-Jordanians and, thus, some Transjordanian-Jordanians who saw the contemporary megaprojects as a means of economic growth and development worried that the development of these projects in the city primarily served Palestinian-Jordanians, but at the expense of Transjordanian-Jordanians. Hence the comments a blogger posted on the Sanaya Amman development who complained that the state spent more money on large-scale projects in the city, particularly the wealthy West Amman, leaving educational and health facilities in other Jordanian cities and towns underdeveloped ("Would you buy," 2008). The comments were exaggerated and evidence could in fact be provided for the state's concern about the development of urban and rural areas in cities other than Amman. However, the connection the blogger made between the state and its spending and the megaprojects was justified considering that major megaprojects in the city were developed by or in partnership with the state. This blogger stated that by embarking on such large-scale developments in Amman, the state disfavored the "native Jordanian," that is, the Transjordanian-Jordanian. He even went so far as to say, "should we just have a country called West Jordan?" This comment implied a connection between West Amman and Palestinian-Jordanians whose roots were in the West Bank, west of Amman. It also showed how the question of identity was strongly related to Amman's early twenty-first-century megaprojects.

There was no evidence that the Palestinian-Jordanian constituency bene-fited, or would benefit, more than other ethnic groups from these large-scale developments. While the private sector in Jordan had more Palestinian-Jordanians than Transjordanian-Jordanians, private developers involved in megaprojects in the city were primarily from outside Jordan. Jordanian firms who were involved in these projects included firms whose ownership belonged to different ethnic groups and whose employees included Jorda-nians from different origins. As for the users of these profit-driven devel-opments, they would include Jordanians from different origins as well as non-Jordanians. What mattered most was not the ethnicity of these users but having the means to spend in such spaces of consumption. These megapro-jects differentiated between city residents in terms of their socioeconomic class rather than ethnicity. And it was hard to make the argument that in the early twenty-first century Transjordanian-Jordanians had fewer means than Palestinian-Jordanians.

Ironically, Amman's megaprojects seemed to have had the potential to symbolically connect the Palestinian in the West Bank with the Jordanian. For example, some individuals noted that the high-rise buildings of the Jor-dan Gate development could be seen from some Palestinian cities, such as Jerusalem (see "One heart," 2009). Jafar Tukan, the principal architect of Jordan Gate who was of Palestinian origin, confirmed that he could see this development from the West Bank (personal communication, July 15, 2010). According to Tukan, Jordan Gate served as a visual connection between the West Bank and Jordan and a reminder of the strong ties between the people of the two countries.

The Muslim Jordanian

Islam is another significant element in the construction of national identity in Jordan. Despite the diverse population of the country, the great major-ity of Jordan's population is Sunni Muslim. Jordan's monarchical dynasty is Sunni Muslim. As descendants of the same Hashemite clan of Prophet

Muhammad and the previous *sharifs* (*sharif* is Arabic for noble and, in this context, the equivalent of a governor) of Mecca and custodians of the Ka'ba, Muslims' most sacred site, the monarchs in Jordan have always identified themselves and Jordan with Islam (see Nasser, 2004; Al Oudat & Alshboul, 2010). In this sense, Jordanians are seen as a part of a bigger Muslim community that believes in one religion: Islam. According to Nasser (2004), during the formative period of the postcolonial state, the 1950s through 1970, official discourse in Jordan identified Jordanianness with Islam, as well as Arabs, much more than it did with Jordan's majority population, that is, the population of Palestinian origin. Nasser argues that this was a strategy for exclusion of the Palestinian majority. But Jordan's identification with Islam would be modified later, as shown in the following sections.

How was the Islamic identity of Amman residents and Jordanians negotiated in the city's early twenty-first-century megaprojects? The most significant feature of the built environment in Amman that connects the city and its residents with Islam is the mosque. The location of King Abdullah I Mosque just east of The New Downtown begs the discussion of the relation between the Abdali development and the mosque and the extent to which this relation emphasizes Islam as an element of the city residents' identification (see Figures 1.4 and 1.5). King Abdullah I Mosque was the most prominent building in this central area of Amman. It was the state congregational mosque that not only had served as a place for prayers and religious celebrations since the late 1980s but also was an icon of Amman, and Jordan, appearing on postcards, tourist promotional material, and TV. This mosque expressed Jordan's identity as Islamic and Jordanians as Muslims; however, rather than responding to King Abdullah I Mosque, the developers disconnected this mosque from The New Downtown.

The planners and architects of the Abdali development talked about visually connecting The New Downtown and King Abdullah I Mosque by organizing this development's components along "visual corridors" that converged toward the mosque (Abdali Investment and Development [AID], n.d.a). But these corridors were not accurately reflected in the organization of spaces and buildings in the Abdali development. One would expect these view corridors to translate into buildings organized along axes that radiated from the mosque, which was not the case as the Abdali site plan shows (Figure 2.8). Earlier Abdali plans included a cultural component, the Civic Pole, linking The New Downtown to the mosque and other state institutions east of the Abdali development (AID, n.d.a). Visually, the Civic Pole's low-rise buildings and open spaces would serve as a transitional zone between King Abdullah I Mosque and the remarkably tall commercial developments in Abdali, reducing the overwhelming impact of these buildings on the mosque and neighboring urban fabric, and the plaza would open up the vista to the mosque. Functionally, the planned Civic Pole would help integrate the mosque, a significant part of the social life in the city, into The New Downtown and, thus, invite city residents from different socioeconomic status to the Abdali development and nurture a sense of belonging and communal as well as national pride. But this cultural component was abandoned at an early stage of the Abdali development and replaced with profit-driven buildings, which closed the development off from and overpowered the mosque, which had once dominated the skyline and landscape of the area.

Some individuals expressed their discontent about the striking contradiction between the scale of buildings in the Abdali development and King Abdullah I Mosque and the likelihood that this development eventually would overwhelm the buildings of the mosque and state institutions neighboring this development (see Figures 2.4 and 2.6). For example, Jawdat said, "the Abdali development is in contrast with its surroundings and its many very tall buildings will eventually dwarf the mosque, which once was considered a large development" (personal communication, January 22, 2010). Dana said, "I don't like that the tall buildings of the Abdali development reduce the size of the mosque and the court of law" (personal communication, February 1, 2010). Similarly, Adham said, "it is unfortunate that the mosque, the landmark of the area, is being superseded by commercial buildings" (personal communication, September 15, 2010). By physically surpassing the mosque, The New Downtown's developers, including the state-owned Mawared, de-emphasized the city's and its population's identification with Islam and asserted the power of and identification with capitalist corporations. The status of King Abdullah I Mosque as the official state mosque was changed when the new King Hussein bin Talal Mosque became the state's official mosque in 2006. Whereas the former was in the center of Amman, the latter was placed in an affluent area on the outskirts of the city. The continued state sponsorship of the state mosque and other mosques, however, showed that the state in Jordan continued to identify with Islam and express it as an element of identification for Jordanians in the built environment, although not in the new megaprojects.

The state mosque was not the only component through which new megaprojects in Amman could connect with the city residents' Islamic identity. Architects working on different developments in The New Downtown incorporated a few elements and features of Islamic architecture, some of which had already become associated with Islam in the minds of Jordanians. However, the rhetoric of these professionals more often than not did not draw a link between such features and Islamic architecture. One of these elements was Islamic ornaments. For example, in the Abdali Boulevard the architects used decorative elements inspired by Islamic calligraphy on the façades of office and residential buildings (Figure 3.1). Similarly, the use

Figure 3.1 Ablaq on the lower part and Islamic calligraphy–inspired decoration on the upper part of a building's façade in the Abdali Boulevard.

Note: Taken by the author on August 9, 2015.

of *ablaq* stone, a decorative technique with alternating courses of light and dark stone, on parts of the Abdali buildings could serve as a connection with Islamic identity (Figure 3.1). In fact, the *ablaq* technique was adopted in the architecture of contemporary mosques in Amman, and it had been used on old mosques of special significance for many Muslim Jordanians.[6] *Ablaq* was a feature commonly used in historic Islamic architecture on sacred and secular buildings, and it became characteristic of Mamluk architecture in Egypt and Bilad al-Sham (the region that included what today are Syria, Lebanon, West Bank, Israel, and Jordan).[7] Although this arrangement of stone was used also on buildings in Western cities, it became associated with Islam. Thus Eldemery (2002) argues that in the award-winning, early twenty-first-century "Future Housing" development, located east of Cairo, the use of *ablaq* on the façades of residential buildings was among the architectural vocabularies that connected this project with Islamic architectural heritage and expressed Islamic identity.

Notwithstanding the few formal connections between early twenty-first-century megaprojects in Amman and features associated with Islamic architecture, and some temporary decorations and shows celebrating Islamic occasions such as Ramadan – the ninth month of the Islamic calendar in which Muslims fast from dawn to sunset – in Abdali's outdoor spaces, there was nothing particularly Islamic about these developments.[8] In fact, a few city residents interviewed for this research viewed these as extravagant developments incompatible with Islamic values of moderation and social equality. For example, Riyad said, "it is inconsistent with Islam to build pretentious developments such as Sanaya Amman, particularly in a low-income neighborhood; it is harmful to people in the neighborhood" (personal communication, September 2, 2013). He added, "why build such gated communities and exclude the poor? Islam does not favor the rich over the poor . . . Islamic values bring harmony among Muslims."

The Arab Jordanian

Identification with Arabs is another significant component of national identity in Jordan where most of the population are Arab. Arabs constitute the majority of the population living in the Arab world, which includes Arabic-speaking countries in the Middle East and North Africa. The majority of Arabs, but not all of them, are Muslim. Despite their diverse economic, political, social, and cultural conditions, Arabs share formal Arabic language, which is comprehensible across the Arabic-speaking world despite dialectical differences. The role language plays in the construction of national identity cannot be overemphasized (see Anderson, 2006), and Arabic was a significant element in the construction of Arab nationalism. Pan-Arabism distinguishes Arabs from others as one political entity with shared history and culture. In this sense, "the [Arab] nation was conceived of as a community speaking the same language, living in the same territory, sharing the same history, and facing the same destiny" (Nasser, 2004, p. 241). Pan-Arabism started to take shape in the early twentieth century and gained momentum after World War II, as a reaction against Ottoman and colonial rule (Nasser, 2004), and it continued through the 1970s.[9]

In the context of Jordan, Amir Abdullah (King as of 1946; r. 1921–1951) hoped to unite Arabs under his leadership. He relentlessly sought unity with Syria and Iraq, but only managed to annex the West Bank to his territory in 1948 (Wilson, 1990). Nasser (2004) argues that during the 1950s through 1970s Jordan identified itself first with the pan-Arab nation, second with Islam, and last with its locality. Like the pan-Islamic identity, the pan-Arab identity also helped establish the legitimacy of Jordan's monarchs because they relate to Prophet Muhammad, who was an Arab (Nasser, 2004). Frisch (2002, p. 100) argues that Jordan's adoption of the pan-Arab identity, particularly under King Hussein (r. 1953–1999), "possesses the additional virtue of attenuating the tension of being a minor state and societal player in the larger Arab region." Emphasis on Arab identity in the official discourse on national identity in Jordan, as well as in many Arab countries, has changed over the past few decades. More often than not, identification with Arabs comes second to the particular identity of the nation-state. Still, Jordan continues to identify itself with the pan-Arab nation, which Frisch (2002) argues will persist while Jordan is a bi-national state consisting of Transjordanians and Palestinians, and while it remains vulnerable to outside threats.

In 2011, the significance of Jordan's identification with Arabs took a new form as Jordan's request to join the Gulf Cooperation Council (GCC) was being considered by GCC members (Halaby, 2011).[10] Contemporary political instabilities in the Arab Middle East were a major force behind Jordan's request (Halaby, 2011). In addition, economic development was a significant impetus behind Jordan's interest in joining the GCC. The relation between political stability and economic situation cannot be overemphasized: a poor economy fuels political unrest. As Halaby points out, a membership in the GCC will boost Jordan's small economy by increasing financial aid from GCC states, opening up Gulf markets to Jordanian exports, and opening up job markets in the Gulf states to Jordanian professionals. In addition, it will increase Jordan's share of Gulf capital investments. In return, Jordan can provide military support to the GCC, an important gain to these countries in a turbulent period (Halaby, 2011). It is still to be seen how national identity in Jordan may be reconstructed if Jordan is admitted to the GCC.

The relation between Amman's megaprojects and Arab identity of the city residents and Jordanians can be investigated through the projects' developers, who were mostly non-Jordanian Arabs. How did Jordanians relate to Arab developers investing in the new megaprojects in the city? One would expect that because officially and popularly Jordanians identify with Arabs, Arab developers would be viewed favorably by the state and the public in

Amman. But this was not necessarily the case. Hoping to enhance the country's economy, the state welcomed Arab developers from the Gulf states who had extra capital to invest in Amman, and other cities in the country. For these developers, Amman, and Jordan, served as an extension to their national territory, which could not absorb excess capital. The public in Amman were not always as welcoming as the state was to the opening up of the city to Gulf developers and their increasing investment in megaprojects. Individuals interviewed over the course of this research had different views with regard to Arabism as a common element of identification between Gulf developers and Jordanians. Interestingly enough, non-Jordanian interviewees, including Arabs and non-Arabs, tended to understand Gulf developers' investment in Amman's urban built environment as reinforcing of Arab ties and identity. Many Jordanians, however, did not understand Gulf developers' investment in megaprojects in the city as reinforcing of Arab ties or Arab identity, and many did not favor Arab over non-Arab developers. Some believed Jordanian developers were as unlikely as Gulf developers to be loyal to the city, and Gulf developers were unlikely to be loyal to the city simply because they were Arabs. For them, capital had no nationality under globalization.

Still, some individuals were concerned about the involvement of non-Jordanians in Amman's contemporary megaprojects. For example Dana said, "so far, the influence of foreign developers on the city has been not good; they control the city" (personal communication, February 1, 2010). Similarly, Fatima said, "I know it may be good to encourage foreign investment, but developers from outside Jordan should not be so influential [in shaping the city]. . . . As foreigners, the moment they find a better place for investment they will leave the country" (personal communication, February 3, 2010). Some expressed their worries that the new megaprojects were disconnected from Jordanians and their socioeconomic conditions and seemed to have been designed for some other "unknown people" from outside Jordan (personal communications, October 2010). One Transjordanian-Jordanian interviewee commented, "these megaprojects could have made sense if the population in Amman were replaced" (personal communication, January 2010). As innocent as these comments might have been, they were sensitive in the context of Jordan. At least half of the country's Jordanian population and the majority of Amman residents were of Palestinian origin, and the relationship between Palestinian-Jordanians and Transjordanian-Jordanians was not always without tension. Some Transjordanian-Jordanians feared that Jordan could become the substitute homeland for the Palestinians who lost Palestine to Israel in the aftermaths of the 1948 and 1967 Arab-Israeli wars. This fear was fueled by Israeli claims in the 1980s that historically Jordan was a part of Palestine and that Palestinians should move to Jordan and establish the Palestinian state there, thus solving the Palestinian-Israeli conflict (see Robins, 1989). In the context of Amman's early twenty-first-century megaprojects, the source of threat to the Jordanian identity was not the Palestinian-Jordanian other, against whom the Transjordanian-Jordanian had identified himself or herself, as much as it was the foreign developer. This threat was considered so serious as reflected in one interviewee's comment that Amman was being "invaded by outsiders in the hand of whom laid its future" (personal communication, October 2010). Some city residents publicly expressed their concern and discontent about the Gulf developers' ownership of land and property in Amman, and in Jordan, which they understood as selling the city and country to these developers ("Investment boom," 2008). In response to this situation, the king stated that Jordan needed to attract investments from the Gulf to boost its small economy, assuring the public that Jordan's national identity would not be compromised ("Investment boom," 2008).

The modern Jordanian

In 2002, Jordan launched the national campaign "*Al-Urdun Awwalan*" (Jordan First), which was "a new outlook on the concept of national identity" in the country (Al Oudat & Alshboul, 2010, p. 87). Jordan First gives priority to the interests of Jordan and its people over regional concerns. However, the Jordanian government remains keen to confirm the country's continuous identification with Arabs and Islam, as the official document on the Jordan First campaign states (King Abdullah II, 2002). Underlying this campaign is concern about Jordan's economic development (Al Oudat & Alshboul, 2010). The campaign also addresses political reform and social development. The Jordanian government sees Jordan First as a means to encourage the nurturing of democracy, equality, "rule of law, public freedom, accountability, [and] transparency" (Embassy of the Hashemite Kingdom of Jordan, n.d.). Furthermore, Jordan First is a means to enhancing patriotism and accommodating the diverse population while maintaining the unity of Jordan (George, 2005; Al Oudat & Alshboul, 2010).

Official discourse promotes Jordan First as an "instrument of modernization" (Al Oudat & Alshboul, 2010, p. 87). This modernization project can be understood as a means to produce Jordanians as a modern nation and individuals like modern nations and individuals of the developed world – a nation and individuals who have ideals of development and standards of comfort similar to those of their counterparts in the developed world, as well as urban built environments and infrastructure that support these ideals and standards and enable economic progress. These universal standards and ideals of modernization had emerged from the West. This is not to equate modernization with Westernization, which as Huntington (1996) pointed out would be simplistic. Adopting modernity does not necessitate embracing the Western culture that produced it, and different nation-states could produce varied modernities (Huntington, 1996). In fact, many Amman residents see themselves as modern and, for them, being modern does not mean breaking with their identity as Muslims, Arabs, tribes, or others. Jordanians formed hybrid modernities in which characteristics from Western and non-Western modernities were adapted and became one dimension of the multiple dimensions of the Jordanian identity. How then did Amman's early twenty-first-century megaprojects contribute to the expression and construction of the modern identity of the city residents and Jordanians?

The new megaprojects in the city can be understood as a means and a product of the modernization project of Jordan and Amman. The developers of The New Downtown and their architects and planners were explicit about the role of this development in constructing and representing the modern city, country, nation, and individual. Thus, according to these developers, the impact of Abdali on the economy of Amman and the country would be assessed based on, among other things, its "creation of a 'physical presence' to a vision" (AID, n.d.a, p. 4). Illustrating this point, they wrote, "the development of a modern city center would be a major tangible achievement on [the] drive towards modernization of the city and the country" (AID, n.d.a, p. 4). The developers considered The New Downtown "an accomplishment that [made] Jordanians proud of always aiming higher and reaching further" ("Project focus," 2009). The #LOVEJO large-scale sculpture, which the developers installed in 2015 in the Abdali Boulevard, can be understood, at least partly, as a means to boost the constructed patriotic role of Abdali while connecting this development with, and to, social media. After all, for the developers, Abdali was an accomplishment that moved Jordan into the twenty-first century "as a solid and strong country" ("Project focus," 2009). Following the lead of the Abdali developers, a high city official described The New Downtown as "a modern commercial center" similar to those in other "modern cities," and he associated it with big businesses and upscale recreation and shopping ("Interview," 2008). The media, in their turn, emphasized the role of Abdali in modernizing Amman, describing it as "breathing modernity into the center of Jordan," a comment that the Abdali developers were proud to highlight in their discourse about this development ("Executive Magazine highlights," 2008; "Jordan – Building Amman's," 2008, para 1). Similarly, many people in Amman, particularly those from the upper-class segment of the society, took pride in The New Downtown, which they found indicative of progress and *hadara*, Arabic for civilization (personal communications, February 2010).

Advertising discourse on Abdali and other contemporary megaprojects in the city contributed to the conception that the city residents were modern, not least because of their association with these new developments. The Abdali developers stated that their advertising campaign would "instill a sense of Jordanian pride" and create a sense of belonging to The New Downtown ("Abdali launches," 2010). In other words, the Abdali advertisements were meant, at least partly, to make the city residents proud of their Jordanianness for having had The New Downtown, which these advertisements described as modern and speaking development (AID, 2008a, 2009). Thus, the Abdali advertisements aimed at unifying under one modern identity the city residents and the nation who had multiple elements of identification. The modern image that the advertisements created for the Abdali, Jordan Gate, and Sanaya developments not only helped construct the megaprojects and city as modern but also served as a medium through which the city residents would understand who they were and how they should live. Thus, some city residents reading the advertisements commented that the megaprojects expressed the modernity of the city residents (personal communications, January 1 and 19, October 7, 2010).

The technologically advanced

In order to express modernity, megaprojects in the city incorporated features associated with the urban built environment of modern Western cities and prominent non-Western cities that had followed the lead of the West, particularly Gulf cities, which would construct Amman, its residents, and the Jordanian nation at large as modern. One way to create the modern nation was to present it as technologically advanced through the incorporation of sophisticated technologies into the built environment. These technologies were manifested in the megaprojects' tall buildings, new building techniques and materials, and information and communications technologies. By the early twenty-first century, tall buildings had already become signifiers of modernity and technological progress in cities around the world no less because of their association with US cities and America as a modern nation. The United States was a part of the Industrial Revolution and the innovative technologies it produced, which made possible the production of tall buildings. Thus in the late nineteenth and early twentieth centuries, high-rise buildings in American cities expressed the modern technologically advanced American nation. Since then, nations around the world adopted these buildings to mark their modernity (see King, 1996). Tall buildings also became a means to construct modernity, and Gulf cities, particularly Dubai, excelled in utilizing them for this purpose.

In early twenty-first-century Amman, high-rise buildings were conceived to project the Jordanian nation as modern, technologically advanced. It is not surprising, then, that tall buildings constituted the landmarks for The New Downtown and were emphasized as the main component of this development's IT Sector, which was considered the area of the Abdali development with the newest technologies and the one most responsible for creating a modern image for this development, the city, and the country (AID, n.d.a; Figures 1.2, 2.4, and 2.6). The unusual inclined tall buildings of Sanaya Amman also were designed to communicate the message that Jordanians were technologically advanced (Figure 1.8). When Sanaya was begun some city residents applauded it as a modern addition to the city's built environment ("Would you buy," 2008). Developments such as Sanaya, according to these individuals, would help the city grow and evolve, leading city residents to take pride in this iconic modern development ("Would you buy," 2008).

Similarly, the record-breaking high-rise buildings of Jordan Gate were seen by many, even by some of those who criticized them for interrupting the landscape and skyline of the neighborhood and the city, as markers of progress and modernity (Figures 1.1, 1.6, and 2.5). Jordan Gate became the source of pride for some city residents and conveyed the idea that the Jordanian was modern. This can be concluded from the responses of individuals interviewed over the course of this research. For example, Husam said, "tall buildings are a sign of progress and to have a development such as this [i.e., Jordan Gate] in Amman means that Jordanians have taken a step toward progress and modernity" (personal communication, October 12, 2010). He also mentioned that his neighbor in a modest neighborhood in Eastern Amman was so excited about the remarkable height of the buildings of Jordan Gate that he used the construction elevator to go up to the top of these buildings before they were completed and took the stairs on his way down; he, then, went on to tell his neighbors and friends about his exciting experience of these buildings, how tall they were, and how the city looked from above. Similarly, Mohammad said, "only in advanced and foreign countries can you find skyscrapers, because you need high technologies to build them" (personal communication, October 4, 2010). He added, "any visitor to Amman will see that these buildings are similar to skyscrapers in the West and know that Jordanians, as Arabs, are advanced. The progress of any Arab country will show the world that Arabs are modern." Mohammad even interpreted the name Jordan Gate as "Jordan's gateway to modernization."

The building process of Jordan Gate showed that, like other megaprojects in early twenty-first-century Amman, this development did not reflect the real technological status of the city or the country. Nor did it reflect the status of the city's infrastructure or its residents' economic situation. Infrastructure in the city was not equipped to handle such megaprojects. Amman suffered from traffic congestion, lack of public transportation, and scarce water resources. Parts of the city were still not connected to the sewage network; rather, they used septic tanks. The majority of the city residents had modest means and could not afford the upscale lifestyle Jordan Gate promoted, not to mention that many could not afford owning a small humble house or shopping for necessities. Although the architects and some of the engineers who designed Jordan Gate were Jordanian, much of the expertise, equipment, and technologies used in the construction of this development were not Jordanian. In the early twenty-first century, the building industry, including builders, craftsmen, and relevant regulatory institutions in Amman, and the country, had not yet assimilated the new imported building systems, materials, and technologies used in Jordan Gate and other megaprojects in the city. This situation in the case of Jordan Gate contributed to a number of accidents during the construction process. For example, three concrete slabs in one of the high-rise buildings fell down and a part of the construction crane collapsed at the level of the 44th floor, causing safety threats to residents in the neighborhood ("Idarat (Bawwabat al-Urdun)," 2006; Kheetan, 2009). Jordan did not have the expertise or know-how to handle these situations because buildings of such a height were not a part of an evolving building tradition. Thus, following the collapse of floor slabs, the developers appointed an international, not a local, consultant for safety ("Idarat (Bawwabat al-Urdun)," 2006). To fix the crane problem, the expertise of foreign specialists was sought and equipment needed to dismantle the broken crane had to be brought from the UAE ("Bad' 'amaliyyat," 2009; "Khubara' yusun," 2009). One of the members of the committee formed for addressing the concerns for public safety as a result of the crane collapse mentioned that the incident was unprecedented in such a large-scale development in Jordan and there were no specialists in the country that could assess the risks from the crane failure (Kheetan, 2009).

Building materials and technologies and architectural styles of the city's megaprojects were other features that conveyed Jordanians' technological advancement. The façades of the Abdali development's tall buildings, particularly those in the IT Sector, were to express modernity (AID, n.d.a). In the Abdali regulations, the developers were encouraged to reflect a high-tech character through the use of glazed curtain walls, metal elements and cladding, and other materials associated with modernity and technological innovation (AID, n.d.a; see Figures 1.2, 2.4, and 3.2). Similarly Jordan Gate's glass curtain walls and Sanaya's steel-and-glass skybridges, suspended swimming pool, and innovative stone mesh incorporated new building technologies and materials and connected these developments

Figure 3.2 Modern materials and high-tech features of buildings and other structures in the Abdali Boulevard.

Note: Taken by the author on August 9, 2015.

with modernity (see Figures 1.6 and 1.8). Even in smaller developments
in The New Downtown where a traditional material such as stone was recommended as a primary façade material, the modern character was to be
emphasized by using relatively smooth-textured stone with fine uniform

surface patterns (AID, n.d.a), which required the use of advanced polishing machines and electric saws. Roughly finished stone, which signaled traditionalism, was not allowed on the Abdali buildings. According to the Abdali developers, this "rural type" of stone would "carry . . . dust and pollution" and it was incommensurate with "the urban modern image" of The New Downtown (AID, n.d.a, p. 49; p. 52; p. 49). Similarly, canopies and awnings in all buildings in the Abdali development should have a modern character (AID, n.d.a). Like tall buildings, building materials and designs were to express modernity and technological progress to create a modern image for the megaprojects, which would construct the city, its residents, and the nation as modern.

Automated systems of building and security management as well as information and communications technologies in megaprojects in the city were also a significant feature for establishing these developments as modern. For example, the developers emphasized Abdali's technologically advanced systems for remote monitoring of interior space and control of services and appliances in this space, high-speed Internet connections, and triple play bundles that combined TV, phone, and Internet ("A smart city," 2008). The developers highlighted the smartness of The New Downtown, which they considered "the most impressive" feature of this development ("A smart city," 2008). Technologies at Abdali, according to the developers, were "the world's most advanced" and "the wonders of technology," which would make Amman a "leader in the world of communications" ("A smart city," 2008). Obviously, even if the Abdali development included state-of-the-art information and communications technologies, it would not make the city a leader in these technologies because The New Downtown was not a place where information technologies were produced, rather it was where these technologies were consumed. This is not to mention that the Abdali development was but a part of a large city in which many residents had no access to such advanced technologies. However, Abdali, like other megaprojects in Amman, was meant to image Amman as a modern city with good information and communications technologies. The naming of a section of this development as the "IT Sector" can be understood in this light of the Abdali development's role in constructing modernity. Considering that the country had an emerging information and communications technologies industry (Henry & Springborg, 2010), emphasis on these technologies in the Abdali development is even more understandable. The IT Sector and the information and communications technologies used in Abdali presented the yet to be developed sector of the country's industry as completely developed industry and the city and nation as modern and technologically advanced.

The modern consumer

The commodified spaces of Amman's contemporary megaprojects (discussed in Chapter 2) help shape the city residents into modern consumers and communicate the message that Jordanians have consumption patterns and lifestyles similar to those of wealthier modern societies in the West and East. Here, the advertisement of megaprojects plays no less a significant role than the development themselves. The modern image of the megaprojects, which the advertisement creates, enhances the appeal of these developments' upscale commodified spaces, induces city residents into consumption, and helps fashion Ammanis into consumers. Williamson (1978) argues that advertising commodifies signifiers and links them to products, the possession of which allegedly will directly give the user the desired quality. This argument can be extended to Amman's megaprojects. The images and texts of the Abdali advertisements present the components of this development as spectacular buildings and landscapes, high-end office spaces, luxury apartments and hotels, and, more important, upscale entertainment and shopping spaces that the city residents, as well as others, need to consume in order to achieve the high social status, joyfulness, and other qualities these spaces signify. Thus, the advertisements not only will "bring people closer to the Abdali project" and allow them to "live the opportunities" and "experiences" of this development, as the developers' comments on these advertisements suggest ("Abdali launches," 2010), but also these advertisements induce city residents into consumption and help make them modern consumers. These city residents will consume commodities and spaces, which became commodities, similarly to the residents of modern cities. And like residents of modern cities, they will seek to build their image through consumption of such commodities, which are after all images signifying favorable qualities. Thus, the Abdali advertisements, which present Abdali as the perfect place for an ideal quality of life, speak of the "individual's self-image" as being "based on the quality of his or her daily life" (AID, n.d.b). According to these advertisements, those who will work, live, shop, or entertain at The New Downtown will be "actively participating in a thriving lifestyle shared by thousands of visitors and residents" (AID, n.d.b).

A telling example of the advertisements' inducement of city residents into consumption is the advertisement of shopping spaces in the Abdali development unsurprisingly titled "Experiences You Desire," a title that represents these spaces as something for which people longed (AID, 2010a; Figure 3.3). The image, which, as in other advertisements of Abdali and large-scale developments in the city, dominates the advertisement, shows a woman with a big smile on her face gazing at a store window in which are reflected images of other good-looking happy female shoppers. No man appears in this image. Instead, men appear in the images of the advertisements on the

Abdali development's office spaces. The Abdali advertisements associate men with work and business and women with shopping and recreation activities, thus reinforcing the idea that men are economic providers and women are dependent on men. All six women in the image of the "Experiences You Desire" advertisement are dressed in fashionable modern clothes; one of the women in the background of the image wears a head cover. This does not represent the real situation in the city where a great number of women cover their heads, and some wear *jilbabs* (loose-fitting dresses that cover the whole body except the head, hands, and feet). Instead, the advertisement's image projects a "modern" image of the Jordanian woman dressed similar to that of the modern woman in the West to enhance the modern image of The New Downtown and the city. Furthermore, this image communicates the message that the Abdali development is a place that will bring to those who will shop its stores and wander its spaces happiness, joyfulness, and all the good qualities associated with modernity. Likewise, the advertisement's text depicts the Abdali development as the perfect place for shopping and entertainment, referring to it as "the best that Amman has to offer." The advertisement speaks of Abdali's "dynamic and stylish venues," "vibrant shopping environment," and brand-name stores, including those at the Abdali Mall and Abdali Boulevard – the two major shopping facilities in this development.

Similarly, the advertisements of Jordan Gate promote this development as "the newest up market [*sic*] district for shopping" (Bayan Holding, Gulf Finance House, & Kuwait Finance and Investment Company, 2007) where "the world's favorite brands will vie for [the visitors'] attention," providing "prestigious, new retail experience" (Jordan Gate Company, n.d.). The Sanaya advertisements also speak of this development's "spacious retail floors," which are "luxurious" and "exclusive" (Limitless, n.d.a). Sanaya's retail area, according to the advertisements, includes "internationally renowned stylish boutiques" (Limitless, n.d.b) and "high end stores" (Limitless, n.d.a), which feature "the latest designers" (Limitless, 2009a). The advertisements note that the Sanaya plaza and side street cafés will "invite" those living in Sanaya and the city residents to this development's shopping and dining spaces (Limitless, n.d.b). The advertisements also speak of Sanaya offering its visitors a "multitude of culinary experiences to choose from": "high-end restaurants," "romantic cafés," and "fast food chains" (Limitless, n.d.a). Such experiences would have come with a high price tag; even fast-food meals from chain restaurants such as McDonald's and KFC are a luxury for many city residents.

The advertisements further lure the readers to become consumers of the city's megaprojects. Thus, Jordan Gate is the "most favored destination for elite shoppers" (Bayan Holding et al., 2007); Sanaya will provide the visitors with "a lifestyle experience" (Limitless, n.d.b); Abdali has "something for everyone" looking for "lively entertainment, fine dining, family events . . . and more" (AID, 2010a). The advertisements present new

Figure 3.3 Advertisement of shopping spaces in the Abdali development (2010).

Note: Reprinted with permission from Abdali Investment and Development and Leo Burnett Jordan.

standards of living that many in the city cannot afford as the standards city residents should adopt to achieve the happiness and satisfaction modern societies enjoy. The advertisements do not express the needs of the city residents and their identities as consumers as much as they create these needs and help fashion the city residents into consumers of the megaprojects' upscale commodified space to serve the interests of the developers, other capitalists engaged in these developments, and the capitalist system in general. It is not surprising, then, that many city residents interviewed about the megaprojects' advertisements said they were excited about shopping and dining spaces at these developments. These were not only from the upper-class segment of the society but also included middle-class individuals who said they would enjoy visiting shopping and entertainment spaces at these developments where they could have a cup of coffee, window-shop the stores, shop for designer clothes during the sale season, or purchase other upscale commodities sold there. Working-class individuals were intimidated by the advertisements' emphasis on the exclusiveness of the advertised spaces. However, some of these did not exclude themselves completely from participating in the upscale megaprojects as can be concluded from Sherif's comment that he would be "just looking" at the Jordan Gate development and the commodities sold there (personal communications, September 30 and October 4, 2010).

Another way the advertisements of megaprojects induce city residents into consumption and shape them into consumers is through the advertisement of residential spaces in these developments. Here, the Abdali advertisement "Lifestyle You Aspire To" is a good example (AID, 2010b; Figure 3.4). As the title suggests, this advertisement manipulates the desires and tastes of the reader. It presents the upscale lifestyle of consumption to which the Abdali development caters as the "new and vibrant way of life," which city residents, as well as others, should seek to achieve high status, happiness, and other good states and attributes. The image of the advertisement shows a smiling woman dressed in modern clothes standing in a luxurious living room next to a floor-to-ceiling corner window talking on her cell phone. Reflections of this woman and a young girl enjoying leisure activities appear on the glass panes. According to the advertisement text, living spaces in the Abdali development made within one's reach "everything . . . [one] could ever imagine in a home." The advertisement does not mention that these spaces come with a price tag that makes them beyond the reach of most people in the city. This advertisement associates Abdali residential spaces with luxury, health, and comfort. Thus, it speaks of these spaces having "important amenities." It speaks of the landscaped and pedestrian areas around the residential buildings supporting an "active, healthy lifestyle." The advertisement also emphasizes the close proximity of these residential spaces to shopping and entertainment spaces in the Abdali development.

Figure 3.4 Advertisement of residential spaces in the Abdali development (2010).

Note: Reprinted with permission from Abdali Investment and Development and Leo Burnett Jordan.

Like the Abdali advertisements, the Sanaya advertisements encourage the city residents to consume upscale residential spaces in the new megaprojects. Sanaya, according to the advertisements, will define a "new era of residential developments" (Limitless, n.d.a) and set "new standards in luxury living" (Limitless, n.d.b). Had this development been realized, these statements would have been true in the context of Amman, and Jordan in general, but not in the regional or global context. Sanaya Amman, as well as The New Downtown, was conceived as a spectacular upscale consumerist space, which was an approach developers of megaprojects adopted worldwide. Producing the urban built environment as a fetishized commodity for consumption, particularly under contemporary globalization processes, followed the logic of capital where capitalists continuously pursue profit. Although Sanaya did not materialize, its advertisements played a role in promoting an upscale lifestyle in which the image and commodity consumption were most significant as the new normal lifestyle of the city residents. This new lifestyle was pitched as the lifestyle appropriate for twenty-first-century modern societies; the lifestyle that would bring all the best to the city and its residents. Thus, when the Sanaya advertisements asked the city residents to "be part of Jordan's new icon of the 21st century" (Limitless, 2009a, 2009b), they called on them to become consumers of Sanaya's spaces and commodities.

To make the residential apartments at Sanaya, as well as Abdali, appeal more to the public, the advertisements speak of them providing security for the residents (AID, 2010b; Limitless, n.d.a). Although Amman was relatively safe, the advertisements posed security as a problem in order to answer the imagined need in the residential apartments. Thus, the Sanaya advertisements highlight this development's "smart building management system" and "in-house dedicated team of door guards, security guards, and supervisors" (Limitless, n.d.a). Such security measures, according to the advertisements, will provide Sanaya residents and visitors with "24-hour peace of mind" (Limitless, n.d.a). Similarly, the Abdali advertisements mention this development's life safety system (AID, n.d.b) that allows residents to remotely "monitor motion in the house against intruders" (AID, 2008b).

The advertisements emphasize the smart technologies incorporated into the megaprojects to further encourage the city residents to become consumers of these developments. Thus, the Sanaya advertisements note this development's cutting-edge, state-of-the-art smart technologies, which were utilized for maximum satisfaction and convenience of Sanaya residents as well as visitors (Limitless, 2009c). The advertisements pitch this development's "smart home automation system," which, through the use of web-based software that meets modern-day needs, will enable Sanaya residents to remotely monitor and control power consumption at their apartments (Limitless, n.d.a). Similarly, the Abdali advertisements speak of this development's smart systems "simplify[ing] every aspect of daily life" and introducing "a new way of living" (AID, 2008b). These practical systems, according to the advertisements, will allow the Abdali residents to "indulge in every comfort, entertainment, and security that technology . . . allowed" (AID, 2008b). The advertisements portray pictures of the comfort and entertainment the Abdali technologies promise. Thus, they speak of the Abdali housewives remotely monitoring the appliances at home as they stroll in the open spaces of the Abdali development and the Abdali residents turning on the air conditioning before they get back home or turning off the lights after they have left home. They speak of residents playing outside not worrying about missing their favorite TV show as it will be available on demand at home "when they get tired from playing" (AID, 2008b).

Advertisement of the leisure amenities and sport facilities at the new megaprojects in the city induces city residents into consumption and plays a role in fashioning them into consumers. The Jordan Gate advertisements speak of this development's leading-edge gymnasium and its facilities and equipment needed for maintaining a healthy lifestyle and sound mind and body (Jordan Gate Company, n.d.). The advertisements present Jordan Gate's leisure spaces as the places for the socially distinguished and the "most desired leisure destination for hard workers to unwind" (Bayan Holding et al., 2007). The Jordan Gate advertisements lure city residents to become consumers of this development's leisure spaces by associating them with eliteness and accomplishment. Exercising at Jordan Gate's world-class gymnasium and relaxing at its luxurious leisure facilities allegedly will assume for the city residents a high social status along with all the good qualities befitting it. Similarly, experiencing Sanaya's leisure amenities, according to this development's advertisement, will attest to the "distinctive living at Sanaya Amman, where dreams become reality" (Limitless, n.d.a). The advertisements' images and texts portray the joyful refreshing experience Sanaya residents will have as they kick off their day with a dip in this development's pool, which the advertisement pitches as "the world's highest suspended swimming pool," and enjoy the "majestic views" of the city's landscape and its clear sky, which the glazed pool offers (Limitless, n.d.a; also see Limitless, n.d.b, 2009a). The advertisements highlight Sanaya's steam rooms, saunas, and Jacuzzis, which will provide Sanaya residents with "an escape from city life" (Limitless, n.d.a). By presenting these facilities as signifiers of well-being and much needed resting, refreshment, and rejuvenation (Limitless, n.d.a), the advertisements help establish a lifestyle of upscale consumption as the lifestyle that the city residents should have. Ironically, the city life from which these facilities were supposed to be an escape would have been integral to the experience of Sanaya residents because Sanaya was to be located in a central area of the city, a location that the advertisements applaud as exclusive. In other words, the Sanaya advertisements depict the city as the best place for living to increase this development's symbolic capital. At the same time, these advertisements suggest the city life is stressful and unsafe to establish the Sanaya development with its leisure amenities and security measures as the ideal place for living in the city.

Advertisement of Sanaya and other contemporary megaprojects encourages the city residents to become consumers of upscale commodified spaces by representing the city's landscape and skyline as a key attraction. Thus, the Sanaya advertisements emphasize the view of landscape from this development's apartments, which they describe as "stunning," "breathtaking," and "unparalleled" (Limitless, n.d.a, 2009a, 2009c). They speak of the distinctive height of the Sanaya buildings and the apartments' floor-to-ceiling windows, balconies, and terraces, all of which will make it possible for the Sanaya residents to capture the "scenic," "panoramic" views of the city (Limitless, n.d.a, n.d.b, 2009a, 2009c). Similarly, the advertisements of Jordan Gate highlight the height of the Jordan Gate hotel and office buildings and their glazed façades as well as the location of this development on a site that has one of the highest elevations in the city, which offers thrilling expansive views of the city's landscape (Bayan Holding et al., 2007; Jordan Gate Company, n.d.). The Abdali advertisements even put more emphasis on the view from buildings. Thus, the image of the advertisement "Lifestyle You Aspire To" shows large glass panes revealing a good part of the city's built environment (Figure 3.4). The advertisement speaks of the Abdali high-rise residential apartments "overlooking a stunning skyline" of the city, which will enable the Abdali residents to "see Amman with a new perspective." Similarly, the advertisement "Experiences You Desire" pitches the "breathtaking roof tops" at the Abdali development. On these rooftops, the Abdali visitors will engage in the consumption of leisure commodities, gazing at the city's architecture and landscape. The views that the advertisements of Amman's contemporary megaprojects depict do not necessarily reflect how the view from the buildings will look in reality, because as Dovey (1999) rightly points out, more often than not, competition for the tallest building and the best view from the building will result in buildings blocking the view they have sought. Instead, these views were imagined to help increase the symbolic capital of the advertised developments.

In the early twenty-first century, identity in Jordan was multidimensional. Official identity was constructed with reference to tribes, Islam, Arabs, and modernization. Popularly, Jordanians identified with different ethnic groups and socioeconomic classes, Islam and Christianity, and Arabs and non-Arabs. Some regarded themselves as modern; others as traditional. Some oscillated between modernity and tradition at different times and in different situations; some defined themselves as simultaneously traditional and modern. Sabry (2010) recognizes this tension between the identification as modern or traditional and the coexistence of tradition and modernity among young Arabs, arguing that many "insist on being both modern and traditional" (p. 19). They believe that "being modern does not and should not necessarily mean parting with tradition, morality or God" (Sabry, 2010). Early twenty-first-century megaprojects in Amman did not reflect this tension between modernity and tradition. Nor did they engage the multiple dimensions of the city residents' identity. These megaprojects primarily connected with modernity, but not with modernity as adapted by the city residents or Jordanians. The new megaprojects and the advertisement that accompanied them collectively presented Ammanis, and Jordanians, as technologically advanced and modern consumers like their counterparts in modern Western and non-Western cities. The technologies these megaprojects incorporated and the consumption patterns they encouraged and helped establish did not reflect the city residents' capabilities, needs, or socioeconomic or cultural condition; rather, they were imported, primarily from the Gulf states and the West.

The new megaprojects in Amman were a part of the official construction of Jordanianness at the turn of the millennium as evident in the agency of the state and city in the production of these developments. Greater Amman Municipality overlooked building regulations, eased licensing processes, and set new building regulations to allow the construction of contemporary megaprojects. The military-owned Mawared was a partner in developing the largest megaproject in early twenty-first-century Amman, The New Downtown. Like the military in other nation-states, the Jordanian military was one of the most significant institutions that created national identity. As Massad (2001) pointed out, the Jordanian military in the colonial and postcolonial states had generated a set of practices, rules, habits, and orders that aimed at normalizing and controlling its members. Not only did the military produce the disciplined soldier, but also it produced the disciplined citizen (Massad, 2001; Mitchell, 1988). The military permeated civic society as its discipline was adopted by other state institutions and the discourses it generated were disseminated through public schools and the media (Massad, 2001; Mitchell, 1988). The military had repressed some cultural material and practices and produced others as the national cultural products, and produced the Jordanian as primarily tribal or Bedouin (Massad, 2001). At the turn of the millennium, however, the modern Jordanian was more in sync with Jordan's modernization and the democratic processes it promoted. Thus the military helped construct the Jordanian as modern, technologically advanced and consumer, partly through investing in a megaproject such as The New Downtown.

Corporate developers from the Gulf states, as well as other developers whose capital was made there or penetrated by Gulf capital, were a major agent in projecting the Jordanian as modern through the new megaprojects they produced in Amman. These developers' willingness to invest in the city's urban built environment encouraged state and city officials, who did not have the money to embark on such megaprojects, to push hard toward reimaging the city and reconstructing its residents' identity. In addition, these developers had great agency in the shape, components, and functions of Amman's megaprojects, as well as in the content of the discourses on these developments, which not only created the city's commodified space and its new image but also helped fashion the lifestyle of Jordanians and their identities in ways that served capitalists' interests rather than the public good. The agency of the architects and planners was also obvious in defining the Jordanian identity through Amman's megaprojects as these professionals shaped the image of the developments and through them the image of the city, consequently influencing the city residents' identity. However, these architects and planners based their designs on the developers' design program and guidelines and, sometimes, conceptual designs and design regulations, which limited design alternatives and made design and planning professional less powerful agents. The public in Amman lacked agency in the communication and construction of their identity through contemporary megaprojects in the city. After all, they were not given a means for input into the production of the modern image and commodified space of the megaprojects or the city at large. But as consumers of the megaprojects' spaces, merchandise, and services, they play a role in consolidating their identity as modern consumers.

Given the strong agencies of corporations, the state, and the city in the production of Amman's new megaprojects, it is not surprising that these developments created the identity of the city residents in ways that connected Jordanians to the modern world and its capitalist economy. Considering the political condition of the time and the economic integration in a global world, the modern Jordanian seemed more appropriate than the Arab, Muslim, or tribal Jordanian for a country and a city seeking financial assistance, foreign investment, and regional as well as international businesses. Furthermore as a modern consumer, the Jordanian will become an agent in perpetuating the capitalist system of production, thus making Jordan more likely to attract businesses. The modern Jordanian identity along with the modern image and commodified space of the city, which the new megaprojects produced, served capitalists' interests and furthered the construction of Amman as a global city.

Notes

1 For example, Massad (2001) shows how Jordanianness was defined differently at Jordan's different historical moments: sometimes it was opposed to the Syrian, Iraqi, Palestinian, and British others, sometimes to the British other, and other times to the Palestinian other.

2 The West Bank is the area of Palestine that was not occupied by the Israeli army at the conclusion of the 1948 Arab-Israeli War.

3 The 1970 civil war between the Jordanian army and the Palestinian guerrillas is another significant reason for this distinction between the Jordanian and the Palestinian other. At the conclusion of this war, the guerrillas were defeated and a campaign of Jordanization was launched (Massad, 2001; Al Oudat & Alshboul, 2010). To this may be added that the very existence of Palestinian refugee camps in Jordan continues to remind Jordanians of the Palestinian other.

4 Alon (2007) argues that the cooptation of tribesmen in the military during the formative years of the state was among the means the state adopted to avoid their threat to the state, to the British, and to Amir Abdullah (King as of 1946; r. 1921–1951). According to Alon, the tribes were not always a source of threat to the state in its formative years. At times tribes cooperated with the state, but at others they resisted it. Their resistance, however, aimed at influencing the state and competing for resources, rather than at overturning it (Alon, 2007).

5 The Abdali website features pictures of the event highlighting Bedouin heritage (see Abdali Investment and Development [AID], 2015).

6 These include Abu Darwish Mosque (completed 1961) in Eastern Amman, which became known as Ablaq Mosque because of the extensive use of stripes of black and white stone all over its façades, and Husseini Mosque (completed 1920s) in downtown Amman, which was the first state mosque and where *ablaq* was used primarily on window and door openings as well as arches.

7 Mamluks ruled Bilad al-Sham and Egypt between 1250 and 1517.

8 For more on Ramadan in Abdali, see "Ramadan at the Boulevard" (2014). Like Ramadan and Eids – Muslim festivals – Christmas and New Year's Eve are celebrated in The New Downtown (see "New Year's Eve," 2015).

9 Regardless of Arab states' official emphasis on pan-Arab identity, Arabic language and cultural products in the Arab world, including movies and music, continue to be a source of unification among Arabs.

10 Founded in 1981, the GCC includes the six oil-rich Arab Gulf states: Bahrain, Kuwait, Oman, Qatar, Saudi Arabia, and United Arab Emirates.

References

Abdali Investment and Development (AID). (n.d.a). *Abdali – A New Downtown for Amman: Sector regulations brief, Sector 1: IT Sector.*

Abdali Investment and Development (AID). (n.d.b). Abdali Downtown: The New Downtown of Amman – A modern landmark in the making [Advertorial; obtained from AID].

Abdali Investment and Development (AID). (2008a). The downtown comes soaring to life. Witness its rise [Advertisement; obtained from AID].

Abdali Investment and Development (AID). (2008b, October). A smart city for a smarter lifestyle - Abdali: A downtown ahead of its time [Advertorial]. *Jordan Property*, 2–3.

Abdali Investment and Development (AID). (2009, May). [Advertisement on the Abdali development]. *Jordan Property*, inside front cover.

Abdali Investment and Development (AID). (2010a). Experiences you desire [Advertisement; obtained from AID].

Abdali Investment and Development (AID). (2010b). Lifestyle you aspire to [Advertisement; obtained from AID].

Abdali Investment and Development (AID). (2015). Jordanian cultural event. Retrieved March 27, 2016, from http://www.abdali.jo/index.php?r=media.

Abdali launches campaign. (2010). *Abdali Newsletter, 10*, 5.

Alon, Y. (2007). *The making of Jordan: Tribes, colonialism and the modern state.* New York: I. B. Tauris.

Anderson, B. (2006; first published 1983). *Imagined communities: Reflections on the origin and spread of nationalism* (2nd ed.). London: Verso.

Bad' 'amaliyyat fakk rafi'at (Abraj al-Urdun) wa al-ahali yarfudun al-rahil [Dismantling of the crane of (Jordan Towers) begins and the neighbors refuse to evacuate; in Arabic]. (2009, May 31). *Al Rai.*

Bayan Holding, Gulf Finance House, & Kuwait Finance and Investment Company. (2007, September). Jordan's highest landmark [Advertisement]. *Jordan Property*, inside back cover.

Çinar, A. (2007). The imagined community as urban reality: The making of Ankara. In A. Çinar & T. Bender (Eds.), *Urban imaginaries: Locating the modern city* (pp. 151–181). Minneapolis: University of Minnesota Press.

Department of Statistics. (2016). Taqrir al-nata'ij al-ra'isiyya lil ti'dad al-'am lil sukk'an wa al-masakin 2015 [Report on main results of population and housing census 2015; in Arabic]. Retrieved June 25, 2016, from http://census.dos.gov.jo/wp-content/uploads/sites/2/2016/02/Census_results_2016.pdf.

Dovey, K. (1999). *Framing places: Mediating power in built form.* London and New York: Routledge.

Eldemery, I. (2002, March). *Islamic architecture: Cultural heritage and future challenges.* Paper presented at the First International Conference of the UIA-WPAHR-Von Architecture and Heritage as a Paradigm for Knowledge and Development: Lessons of the Past, New Inventions and Future Challenges, Alexandria, Egypt.

Embassy of the Hashemite Kingdom of Jordan – Washington, D.C. (n.d.). Timeline of political reform. Retrieved August 16, 2016, from http://jordanembassyus.org/politics/timeline-political-reform.

Executive Magazine highlights sustainable development role of Abdali. (2008). *Abdali Newsletter, 6*, 10.

Frisch, H. (2002). Fuzzy nationalism: The case of Jordan. *Nationalism and Ethnic Politics, 8*(4), 86–103.

George, A. (2005). *Jordan: Living in the crossfire.* London and New York: Zed Books.

Halaby, J. (2011, May 12). Jordan's GCC membership push offers mutual gains. *Deseret News.* Retrieved August 16, 2016, from http://www.deseretnews.com/article/700134705/Jordans-GCC-membership-push-offers-mutual-gains.html.

Harvey, D. (1989). *The urban experience*. Baltimore: Johns Hopkins University Press.

Harvey, D. (1990). *The condition of postmodernity: An enquiry into the origins of cultural change*. New York: Blackwell.

Harvey, D. (1991). The urban face of capitalism. In J.F. Hart (Ed.), *Our changing cities* (pp. 51–66). Baltimore and London: Johns Hopkins University Press.

Henry, C.M., & Springborg, R. (2010). *Globalization and the politics of development in the Middle East* (2nd ed.). Cambridge, MA: Cambridge University Press.

Hobsbawm, E. (1983). Introduction: Inventing traditions. In E. Hobsbawm & T. Ranger (Eds.), *The invention of tradition* (pp. 1–14). Cambridge, MA: Cambridge University Press.

Huntington, S. (1996). The West unique, not universal. *Foreign Affairs, 75*(6), 28–46.

Idarat (Bawwabat al-Urdun) yu'ayyin istishariyyan 'alamiyyan li al-salama [The management of (Jordan Gates) appoints an international consultant for public safety; in Arabic]. (2006, September 19). *Al Rai*. Retrieved August 16, 2016, from http://www.alrai.com/article/188912.html.

Interview by Mohammad Shamma [in Arabic]. (2008, June 22). *Alghad*.

Investment boom from Gulf petrodollars makes Jordanians leery their nation is being sold out. (2008, July 13). *Herald Tribune*.

Jordan – Building Amman's future: Abdali Urban Regeneration project to transform heart of capital city. (2008, July). *Executive Magazine*.

Jordan Gate Company. (n.d.). Introducing Jordan Gate [Brochure].

Kheetan, T. (2009, May 26). Residents of nearby buildings reject compensation offer. *The Jordan Times*.

Khubara' yusun bi darurat fakk rafi'at al-abraj bi asra' waqt [Experts strongly recommend dismantling of the towers' crane soon; in Arabic]. (2009, May 21). *Al Rai*.

King, A. (1996). Worlds in the city: Manhattan transfer and the ascendance of spectacular space. *Planning Perspectives, 11*(2), 97–114.

King Abdullah II. (2002, October 29). Letter to Ali Abul Ragheb on the national interest. Retrieved August 15, 2016, from http://www.kingabdullah.jo/index.php/en_US/royalLetters/view/id/139.html.

Limitless. (n.d.a). Sanaya Amman [Brochure].

Limitless. (n.d.b). [Video on Sanaya Amman]. *YouTube*. Retrieved August 16, 2016, from https://www.youtube.com/watch?v=K4VnqPNV1dk.

Limitless. (2009a). Sanaya Amman [Advertisement]. *Catalog of the PropertyLink'09 Exhibition: The 4th International Property and Real Estate Investment Exhibition*. May 10–13. Amman: Zara Expo. Back cover.

Limitless. (2009b, May). [Advertisement on Sanaya Amman]. *Jordan Property*, foldout front cover.

Limitless. (2009c, May 9). [Advertisement on Sanaya Amman]. *Amlak*, 9.

Massad, J. (2001). *Colonial effects: The making of national identity in Jordan*. New York: Columbia University Press.

Mernin, A. (2007, February 18). Amman on a mission. *Arabian Business.com*. Retrieved August 15, 2016, from http://www.arabianbusiness.com/amman-on-mission-149078.html.

Mitchell, T. (1988). *Colonising Egypt*. Cambridge, MA: Cambridge University Press.

Nasser, R. (2004). Exclusion and the making of Jordanian national identity: An analysis of school textbooks. *Nationalism and Ethnic Politics, 10*(2), 221–249.

Nevo, J. (2003). Changing identities in Jordan. *Israel Affairs, 9*(3), 187–208.

New Year's Eve at the Boulevard 2016. (2015, December 31). Retrieved August 15, 2016, from http://www.abdali-boulevard.jo/Events/52-New-Year%27s-Eve-at-The-Boulevard-2016.html.

One heart . . . in two bodies. (2009). Retrieved August 15, 2016, from http://mmustafa.wordpress.com/2009/08/23/one-heart/.

Al Oudat, M.A., & Alshboul, A. (2010). Jordan first: Tribalism, nationalism and legitimacy of power in Jordan. *Intellectual Discourse, 18*(1), 65–96.

Parker, C. (2009). Tunnel-bypasses and minarets of capitalism: Amman as neoliberal assemblage. *Political Geography, 28*(2), 110–120.

Project focus. (2009). *Abdali Newsletter, 9*, 5.

Ramadan at the Boulevard. (2014, June 29). Retrieved March 27, 2016, from http://www.abdali-boulevard.jo/Events/25-Ramadan-at-The-Boulevard-.html.

Robins, P. (1989). Shedding half a kingdom: Jordan's dismantling of ties with the West Bank. *Bulletin (British Society for Middle Eastern Studies), 16*(2), 162–175.

Sabry, T. (2010). *Cultural encounters in the Arab world: On media, the modern and the everyday*. London and New York: I. B. Tauris.

A smart city for a smarter lifestyle. (2008). *Abdali Newsletter, 6*, 4.

Susser, A. (2000). The Jordanian monarchy: The Hashemite success story. In J. Kostiner (Ed.), *Middle East monarchies: The challenge of modernity* (pp. 87–116). London: Lynne Rienner.

Williamson, J. (1978). *Decoding advertisements: Ideology and meaning in advertising*. London: Marion Boyars.

Wilson, M. (1990). *King Abdullah, Britain and the making of Jordan*. New York: Cambridge University Press.

Would you buy a flat in Amman's newest 300 million dollar tower? (2008, February 16). *360°east*. Retrieved August 14, 2016, from http://www.360east.com/?p=931.

4 Findings and conclusion

Discussion of the book's key findings and their theoretical implications

In the 2000s, oil-rich Arab Gulf states had capital surpluses, which they could not absorb within their geographical boundaries. The integration of Jordan's economy into the global economy and Gulf economy, which itself has always been an integral part of the global economy, and the late twentieth- and early twenty-first-century economic reform in the country, which was necessitated and reinforced by Jordan's economic integration, along with the country's political stability, proximity to Gulf states, and pleasant weather, attracted excess capital from the Gulf and encouraged foreign investment in Amman in several megaprojects, many of which were unprecedented in the city. Having been globally integrated, the country's economy was hit by the 2008 global economic crisis and urban developments in the city were affected. By the end of the 2000s, some Gulf investors, as well as other investors, had suspended their developments, prospective property buyers put buying decisions on hold in hopes that real estate prices would fall (Oxford Business Group, 2009), many buyers of under-construction property broke contracts after having made advance payments, and construction activity in the city had slowed. During the second decade of the twenty-first century, Gulf capital flows to Amman resumed and construction activity started to pick up, reaching a relatively high level in mid-decade, but not yet matching the level before the economic crisis.

The theorization of Harvey (1989a, 1990, 1994, 2005) is relevant here, that urban transformation can be understood in relation to capitalism and capitalists' search for a spatial solution to the problem of overaccumulation inherent in capitalism. Although Harvey's argument was made in response to advanced capitalism in the West, it proved applicable in the context of this study with respect to the advanced capitalism in the Gulf and the patient capitalism in Jordan. As in Canary Wharf and other projects, capitalists move excess capital that cannot be absorbed in profitable production processes to investment in the urban built environment. But the increasing investment in the production of urban developments, as Harvey (1989a) argues, eventually leads to overinvestment and market saturation, leading back to the problem of capital overaccumulation. It follows, then, that the spatial fix is only a temporary fix for capitalists' problems, and it foreshadows economic collapse. Canary Wharf failed in the early 1990s because it was an example of overinvestment in urban development. Similarly, the failure of some of Amman's megaprojects in the late 2000s and the construction slump that faced other megaprojects in the city can be attributed to overinvestment in urban development in the region. Investment in the urban built environment in the Gulf where capital surplus problem arose was nearing its peak when capital began to be diverted to investment in Amman's built environment. Whereas Canary Wharf had recovered from the economic downturn of the 1980s and was considered economically successful by the early twenty-first century, it remains unknown whether Amman's megaprojects will be viewed similarly after the economic crisis of the 2000s has fully passed.

The study has found that the production of Amman's contemporary mega-projects caused the destruction of buildings and landscapes in the city deemed less lucrative than the new developments. Harvey (1989a, 1990) argues that urban transformation under capitalism, particularly under contemporary globalization processes, follows the process of creative destruction inherent in the capitalist system of production. It is in light of this process that Harvey understands the destruction of factories and docklands in the West in the last quarter of the twentieth century and their replacement with office buildings, shopping malls, and entertainment facilities such as those of the Baltimore and Canary Wharf developments. In Amman, the process of creative destruction occurred with alteration, thus expanding on Harvey's understanding of this process. Urban fabric that had evolved over many decades in response to various economic, political, and sociocultural forces from inside and outside the city was replaced with instant large-scale developments that responded to regional and global economic forces. Among the built environments the process of creative destruction targeted in Amman were military facilities and other public-owned buildings, privately owned residential, educational, and commercial buildings, and a public park. Unlike the abandoned deteriorating factories and docklands in the West, most of the buildings and landscapes in Amman were in use just before they were demolished. But by the turn of the millennium, the price of the land they occupied had increased significantly and developers from outside the country, particularly from Gulf states, were looking for investment in urban developments in Amman. State and city officials were instrumental in replacing existing buildings and landscapes in the city, along with the socioeconomic and cultural activities they supported, with upscale mixed-use megaprojects driven by profit-making, not the needs of the city residents. Lacking democratic processes in the country and city facilitated the process of creative destruction. The public's opinions about the replacement of existing buildings and landscapes with the new megaprojects were not sought and its objection to this transformation was not heard. Another characteristic differentiates creative destruction in Amman from this process in the West. Although in both contexts creative destruction was designed to attract capital, corporations, and tourists, in Amman it was also a means to develop the economy in ways that paralleled other modernization processes underway in the country in the early twenty-first century. The process of creative destruction fulfilled the aspiration for modernity as it involved the replacement of modest buildings and landscapes with spectacular ones similar to those in global cities, thus redefining the city as global and the city residents as modern.

The city's urban built environment shaped over decades was considered incommensurate with the newly defined global Amman. By the early twenty-first century Amman's built environment included unharmonious buildings of different styles, architectural vocabularies, shapes, height, materials, and colors. The International-style buildings of the 1950s–1970s, which once were considered modern buildings, no longer reflected the spirit of the time. Nor were the city's unpretentious, low- and mid-rise stone-clad buildings, or even the luxurious buildings of the 1970s and 1980s, fit for twenty-first-century Amman. Housing projects of the 1970s and public and private educational and health buildings of the 1990s were not the kind of projects that would showcase the globality of the city. To the contrary, the 1990s' upscale commercial high-rise buildings, spectacular buildings finished in glass, aluminum, and other innovative materials, shopping malls, and global fast-food and coffee shop franchises were the kind of developments that developers and decision-makers wanted for twenty-first-century Amman. However, these were to be reproduced at a larger and wider scale and in more spectacular ways than their 1990s' counterparts. Spectacular megaprojects similar to those in global cities, large-scale developments that became markers of modernity and globality, were believed to be a means to construct this Amman. As shown in Chapter 2, these megaprojects would include a downtown speaking progress and modernity such as The New Downtown (Abdali), iconic developments by Western starchitects such as Sanaya Amman, and glazed, record-breaking tall landmark buildings such as Jordan Gate.

Encouraged by foreign investment opportunities in Amman and lured by Gulf capital flows, state and city officials exercised their power to reimage the city as a global city. Late nineteenth- and twentieth-century Amman was a globalizing city continuously shaped by global and regional economic, political, and sociocultural forces. In the early twenty-first century, however, state and city officials sought to construct the city as a global city, a city that was competitive in terms of its global economic integration, international producer-services, and spaces supporting international corporations and financial transactions. These were main indicators of the degree of a city's globality under the limited understanding of globalization as primarily economic processes. Up to the early 2000s, Amman was not a global city as defined by such indicators. Jordan's economic reform and integration combined with the city's new global image, which was being produced partly through the transformation of the city's built environment, led to the inclusion of Amman in 2008 on a list of global cities by the Globalization and World Cities (GaWC) Research Network. Still the city ranked low on this list. Enhancing Amman's global image was a deliberate strategy to place the city higher on the list.[1]

Thus Greater Amman Municipality (GAM) devised the Amman Plan between 2006 and 2008, which encouraged real estate investment in the city in an effort to make it a destination for foreign investors and tourists. The new regulation for high-rise buildings in this plan allowed the development of a megaproject such as Sanaya Amman in the city's wadis. It also legitimized high-rise buildings within The New Downtown, in a central area of the city previously designated for low- and mid-rise developments. Here, the developers included a large number of high-rise buildings, pressuring GAM to change building regulations for the project site accordingly. The partnership between the state-owned Mawared and the private developers Horizon and United Real Estate in Abdali was a strong factor in influencing GAM's regulations and helping the developers reshape the city's built environment. The development of public-private partnership (PPP) in the early twenty-first century as a new approach to business in Amman, as well as the country, helped attract many investors and facilitated the production of several megaprojects in the city. But as the study has found and Daher (2008a) has pointed out, PPP in Amman's megaprojects served the interests of private corporations at the expense of the public. In the case of the Jordan Gate development, the city's partnership with corporate developers even led to the privatization of public space – the park. Such consequences of PPP are not unique to Amman. Stallmeyer (2011) shows how in the case of Divyasree Chambers, one of the largest ICT developments in Bangalore Central Business District, a previous joint venture between private developers and the city made possible the transformation of a former public site into a privately owned development. However, unlike the case of Jordan Gate, the private partner in Divyasree Chambers was local.

Other scholars have identified the effect of PPP in urban developments in Western and non-Western contexts on disenfranchising the public (see Ghosh, 2005; Harvey, 1989b; Makdisi, 1997). Drawing upon the case of urban developments in Baltimore, Harvey (1989b) argues that the partnership between the private sector and local public sector is an essential component of "urban entrepreneurialism," which is concerned more with producing large-scale developments that can enhance the image of the city and attract investment capital, particularly foreign capital, than smaller projects that cater to the needs of local communities. According to Harvey, PPP in the United States subsidizes corporations, taking resources away from the less privileged population and increasing social inequality in the city. Furthermore, more often than not the private sector reaps the benefit from PPP while the public sector suffers the perils that may result from the speculative nature of the developments produced under this partnership. Urban entrepreneurialism applies to Amman, although with modification. The PPP model used in Amman was different from Harvey's model because it operated not only at the level of the city but also at the level of the state, as evident in the Abdali development where the military was a part of this partnership, giving this development legitimacy. With the state as a partner, national resources were diverted to subsidize corporations, and thus failure of any speculative development carried out under this PPP to recoup its costs or generate profit will have an impact at the national level. Here the case of Beirut Central District (BCD) during the first decade of this development's construction is instructive. The Lebanese government, which was a partner with the private sector in the BCD, had to borrow substantial amounts so that it could provide the infrastructure for this development. This left Lebanon with substantial foreign debt, which ultimately would be paid for by the public, particularly the poor because Lebanon had a regressive tax system (Kubursi, 1999; also see Larkin, 2010). Makdisi (1997, p. 672) argues that PPP in the BCD was a "decisive colonization" of the public interests by the private interests. As in Amman, and Beirut, urban development in Dubai is entrepreneurial (see Kanna, 2011). But in Dubai, PPP is not as important a component of urban development as in Amman, Beirut, or Baltimore. Instead, the ruler of the emirate owns many major corporations developing the city's megaprojects (Elsheshtawy, 2010; Kanna, 2011). Corporations owned by Dubai's influential merchants, who are often linked to the government, are also active in urban development in the city (Kanna, 2011). That the ruler of Dubai owns much of Dubai's land further facilitates the production of large-scale developments in the city (Kanna, 2011), which, like their counterparts in Amman, are devised to create a global city image and attract investors and tourists.

Unlike Dubai, in Amman private corporations, particularly Gulf corporations who partnered with the state or city, were a more powerful agent than the state and city in reshaping the city's landscape and constructing global Amman. The state and city needed the capital of these corporations to transform the image of the city. Lack of financial resources in the city, and the country in general, hindered full implementation of the ambitious urban plans proposed for Amman in the second half of the twentieth century. These plans envisaged the downtown with large-scale developments, including high-rise office and hotel buildings and commercial centers, to encourage investment and tourism in the city. The early twenty-first-century New Downtown was reminiscent of the developments proposed for the downtown in the previous plans. As Abu-Dayyeh (2004) points out, parts of the previous plans for the city would eventually materialize, although not necessarily in the originally proposed location.[2] The architects and planners hired by private corporations were another agent, although a less powerful one, in shaping the city's megaprojects and, consequently, the city image.

The city residents had the least degree of agency. They were not allowed to participate in decision-making regarding the function or form of these developments. In a few cases, some city residents tried to resist the power of the developers, state, or city to transform the built environment, but ultimately the developers, state, and city predominated in producing the city's megaprojects. As Harvey (1989a, 1990) argues, the macro-power of capital, capitalists, and the capitalist state is predominant in the production of urban developments. The macro-power of these actors was even more dominant in Amman than in the Western context on which Harvey based his argument. In Amman, as well as many other Arab cities, lack of public participation in urban development can be attributed, at least in part, to the authoritarian power of the state (see Barthel, 2010). The limited exercise of power by individuals and groups of individuals only partly connects with Foucault's (1984/2003) understanding of power as exercised in different social activities and at different levels, including the micro level of the individual. In Amman, the micro-power of the city resident was more at play in the construction of the city image and identity than it was in the production of these megaprojects. The public exercised more power in making sense of and understanding themselves through these megaprojects and the discourses that accompanied them than they did in decision-making regarding the actual production of megaprojects. Still, the public did not always challenge the macro-power of corporations, the state, and the city; when it did, it did not always prevail.

The study has found that image-building was significant in the conception of megaprojects in Amman. As Harvey (1990, 2001) argues, creating a quality image of the urban built environment through the production of

conspicuous buildings and urban spaces is most important in the production of urban developments under contemporary globalization processes.
Thus, as shown in Chapter 2, the developers of Amman's new megaprojects
produced and constructed these projects as spectacular developments that
appealed as much as imagined images as real entities. This was evident, for
example, in The New Downtown's designs in which theatrical buildings
and urban spaces were organized based on view corridors and conspicuous
tall buildings served as landmarks, building regulations in which buildings'
shapes, details, and materials were strictly controlled, and discourses in
which the image was elevated. For the city's megaprojects, the developers
created a modern image that would produce a new image for Amman: an
image deemed fit for the new millennium. This was a global city image,
which, as Olds (1995) argues, is something producers of megaprojects often
seek. In fact, scholars have credited contemporary megaprojects in Dubai –
the city with which Amman and other cities in the region try to compete –
for creating Dubai's global image (see Elsheshtawy, 2004, 2010; Kanna,
2011).

Like other global cities, Amman was to be constructed as the perfect place
for work, living, and entertainment. It was to be created as the place that
primarily catered to international, regional, and national businesspersons,
tourists, and well-to-do individuals. Thus the city's megaprojects included
high-end office, residential, shopping, and entertainment spaces, which
served functions similar to those of megaprojects in globally competitive
cities and portrayed Amman as a first-rate global city to attract corporations,
investors, and visitors. Corporations investing in these megaprojects and
the state and city, who served as co-developers, legislators, or facilitators
of these developments, believed it was more profitable to market, sell, and
consume the city's megaprojects and urban built environment in a global
Amman. For state and city officials, the making of global Amman was a
means to stimulate the city's, as well as the country's, economy and increase
its integration into the global economy; for the private developers, it was a
means to grow their capital.

That the new megaprojects in the city constructed global Amman is in
part consistent with the argument by King (1996) that the city is imaged and
imagined through the built environment. In line with King's argument, the
study finding indicates that buildings and urban spaces shape the city and
create images in the minds of their viewers and users, which became for
them representative of the city as a whole with its complex social, economic,
political, and cultural structure. This study finding, however, is inconsistent with King's argument that because the city residents are unlikely to
visit or know the whole city, the city exists in their minds only and, thus,
it is imagined. Concluding that Amman's megaprojects produced the city

image and global Amman is not to say that the city does not exist. Rather, it means that these megaprojects shaped the built environment and the way people perceived this environment, and created a mental construction of the city, which does not necessarily correspond with the city's reality. In other words, the ideas people form about the city through the built environment, among other things, can be imagined. Still, the physical components of the city, including buildings, urban spaces, and natural landscapes, do exist regardless of how people imagine them or whether or not they will ever visit or know them. This finding connects with Donald's (1999) understanding that the city is both a thing and a state of mind.

Amman's new megaprojects introduced different urban patterns and architectural vocabulary, interrupting the city's landscape and skyline. Since the mid-twentieth century, Amman's built environment had been undergoing increasing transformation. This transformation was influenced by regional and international circulation of images and ideas, the encouragement of transnational investment capital, and hosting refugees and displaced people from neighboring war-affected countries. In the early twenty-first century, however, the city's attraction of capital from the Gulf states and its investment in the built environment played greater role in further intensifying urban transformation. This also increased the dissemination of ideas and images, particularly from the Gulf, and made possible the production of large-scale developments influenced by these ideas and images, significantly reshaping the city's landscape.

Some in the city, including practicing architects, suggested that architects designing for the city in the early twenty-first century imported packaged architectural forms that belonged to different geographical context and forced them into Amman's built environment (R. Badran, personal communication, September 1, 2010; Malkawi & Kaddoura, 2007). This was only partly true. Not all architects and private planners working on the new megaprojects simply copied designs of developments in other cities. After all, some of these architects and planners were established professionals of national or international reputation, and large-scale developments in Amman provided them with an opportunity to showcase their creativity, leave their mark on the city, and boost their portfolio. However, these architects and planners were responding to the developers' design programs and conceptions, which were similar to those of megaprojects in the region and worldwide. In addition, state and city officials sought to realize through these large-scale developments their vision for Amman, a vision where the city was modern and global. This vision was shaped, at least partially, by Dubai's spectacular megaprojects, which enhanced Dubai's status as a modern and global city. It is not surprising, then, that state and city officials were more concerned with producing spectacular, record-breaking, technologically advanced globally recognizable developments than producing developments that connected to the city's architectural tradition.

The designers of the new megaprojects in Amman tried at the same time to distinguish these projects from and maintain resemblance to other global large-scale developments catering to international and regional businesspersons and tourists, among others. Some designers made reference to the city's architectural tradition, but often in a distant and indirect way. The most common strategy was the use of stone on buildings' façades, although not necessarily as the major finishing material or in colors, textures, or patterns similar to those used on buildings that were a part of the city's architectural tradition. For example, the stone mesh on the façades of Sanaya Amman did not connect this development with its significantly tall buildings and glass and steel bridges and swimming pool with the city's landscape, and the stone-clad base of Jordan Gate was inadequate to relate this development with its fully glazed high-rise buildings to Amman's architectural tradition. Although some developments, particularly small-scale developments in The New Downtown, could be considered hybrid, many large-scale developments in early twenty-first-century Amman were unlikely to qualify as hybrid. The scale of these developments, their programs, and, more important, their conception as modern developments similar to those in global cities suggested their divergence from the architectural tradition of the city. But it would be simplistic to say that they looked exactly the same as megaprojects in other cities. More often than not, these developments connected more with the generic megaproject, particularly in Gulf cities, than they did with the particular architecture of the city. One point needs to be emphasized here. The developers of Amman's megaprojects were selective when borrowing from the architecture of the Gulf. Whereas many megaprojects in the Gulf have universal forms, other large-scale developments invoke local or regional architectural tradition or borrow architectural vocabularies from beyond the region.

The study's findings support the argument by Beynon and Dunkerley (2000) that globalization may simultaneously lead to the homogeneity and hybridity of cultural production. The findings are also consistent with the widely accepted scholarly understanding identified by Beynon and Dunkerley that rejects the strong version of the homogeneity of cultural production under globalization. More important, the study's findings indicate that the strong version of the heterogeneity and hybridity of cultural production under globalization does not always apply to the urban built environment, which is an important part of cultural production. After all, the shape and function of Amman's megaprojects were more universal than particular, which is consistent with Harvey's (1990) argument that the opening up of cities to capital accumulation often results in a limited sense of differentiation amid wide similarities in the shape and pattern of built environments in different geographical locations. Harvey (2001) argues that under contemporary globalization capitalists seek a balance between the need to produce urban spaces that are similar to those in other localities so that they will be easily tradable and, at the same time, different enough from urban spaces in other localities so that they will have economic advantage over them. Because urban spaces that are completely different from those in other cities will be untradeable or "outside globalization," to use Harvey's (2001, p. 408) words, there is a tendency to produce built environments with similar spatial patterns and characteristics in different cities. The producers of Amman's megaprojects were keen to produce global developments and construct a global city image for Amman, and thus the megaprojects had wide similarities in their shape and function with megaprojects in other global cities, particularly in the Gulf. The influence of the Gulf on shaping Amman's megaprojects demonstrates that the source of cultural flows under contemporary globalization processes is not limited to the West. However, the influence of the West should not be overlooked because Western architects and planners had helped shape the built environment in Gulf cities, and Western architects, engineers, and other professionals, as well as others who were educated in the West or in institutions modeled after Western universities, played an important role in shaping Amman's megaprojects.

The study has found that, like the megaprojects themselves, the developers' discourse on the city's megaprojects, particularly advertisement, created the image of these projects as outstanding modern developments and constructed Amman as a competitive regional and global city. It did so partly through conveying a modern city image and partly through promoting Amman as a city that had distinguished work, living, and entertainment spaces and was the perfect place for regional and international businesses and the destination for businesspersons and tourists as well as city residents. The role that discourse played in creating a global city image for Amman is consistent with the theorization of Foucault (1969/1972) that discourse produces the objects of which it speaks and shapes reality. It is also in line with Harvey's (2001) understanding that under the global capitalist economy, discourse, including advertisement, is significant for defining products and the built environment.

Not only did Amman's megaprojects, and the discourse surrounding them, construct global Amman, but they were designed to create and communicate a modern identity of the city residents and Jordanians. The constructedness of the Jordanian identity is in line with Anderson's (2006) argument that the nation is imagined and Massad's (2001) argument that the Jordanian identity had been shaped and reshaped over the past decades in response to the country's changing circumstances. As shown in Chapter 3, state institutions defined Jordan's official national identity with reference to four elements: tribes, Islam, Arabs, and modernization. Popularly, Jordanians identified with these elements as well as others, such as different ethnic groups and socioeconomic classes. However, Amman's megaprojects did not connect equally with these elements of identification. These developments primarily connected with modernization, an official discourse that predominated in the country in the early twenty-first century. Many Ammanis, and Jordanians, had identified themselves as modern by the time the country's modernization project was launched and they had adapted modernity and made it an integral part of their Jordanian identity. However, Amman's new megaprojects did not express particular Jordanian modernities.

Here the argument of Lu (2011) about modernity and the urban built environment in developing countries is relevant. In mid-twentieth-century developing countries, according to Lu, modernity was adapted and made into a new modernism: "Third World modernism." This was not an incomplete or imperfect modernity yet to be developed into the Western modernity; rather it was one of the multiple ways of being modern.[3] Lu argued that Third World modernism produced its own architecture, an architecture in which the Western modernity was domesticated. This was not the case in Amman. Only a few scholars argued that Amman's architecture in the 1950s and 1960s reflected a particular Jordanian modernity (see Daher, 2008b), and even these were arguably nostalgic about the built environment they experienced growing up. In the context of Arab cities and their modernity at the turn of the twenty-first century, Asfour (2009) argued that the built environment that reflected modernity satisfied the public's aspiration for the Western modernity and expressed people's identification with this modernity, whereas the built environment that made immediate reference to tradition disconnected from Arab societies who aspired to modernity, not tradition. Asfour failed to recognize the complexity and multidimensionality of identity in the Arab world, which included modernity and tradition, among other things. In addition, he emphasized the expressiveness of identity in the built environment over the constructedness of identity through this environment and, thus, he failed to recognize the agency of the producers of urban developments in shaping identity. If the urban built environment in the Arab world was to express the identity of the city residents, it should have related to the multiple elements of identification of these residents. Similarly, if megaprojects in Amman were to connect with the public in the city, these developments should have reflected the city residents' multidimensional identities. They should have represented and solidified a Jordanian modernity or a range of Jordanian modernities, rather than imposing a modernity on the city and its residents that was not theirs.

The modern and global image that Amman's megaprojects and the advertisements, as well as other discourses, on them created conveyed the message that Jordanians were technologically advanced like their counterparts in modern Western cities and prominent non-Western cities. Building designs, materials, and technologies associated with progress and modernity, such as tall buildings, glass- and metal-clad buildings, and glass-and-steel skybridges, did not express the advancement of Jordanians. Rather, they were employed with the help of foreign expertise to communicate the message that Jordanians were at the forefront of technology and innovation. It is also in this light of projecting a modern Jordanian identity that environment-friendly designs and technologies using Western green building criteria and expertise can be understood. These designs and technologies reflected a particular kind of environmental consciousness and demonstrated that the developers of recent megaprojects in the city were keen to keep up with Western standards. Power-generating wind turbines, stone mesh utilized for water heating, and water-recycling systems were energy- and water-saving measures that conformed to Western standards of Leadership in Energy and Environmental Design (LEED), required Western expertise, and suggested that Jordanians were modern technologically advanced, as well as environmentally conscious.[4]

Amman's contemporary megaprojects were produced as commodified spaces and they, as well as the discourse surrounding them, helped shape Ammanis into consumers. While it is true that a number of developments produced in Amman during the last quarter of the twentieth century were places for consumption, including the shopping malls of the 1990s and the 1970s Housing Bank Center with its iconic building, terraces overlooking the city's landscape, and dining and shopping spaces, in the early twenty-first century the intensity and extensity by which the consumerist space was produced in the city were unprecedented. Furthermore, the commodified space of early twenty-first-century Amman was upscale targeting the city residents, most of whom were of modest means, as well as corporations and individuals from outside the city. In Amman's contemporary megaprojects, the image of high-end buildings, luxurious spaces, and upscale commodities displayed and sold there became the center of attention and an important part of people's everyday lives. Shopping, living, and work spaces became fetishized commodities, attesting to commodity domination of urban social life and the commodification of the city. As Debord (1967/1994) argues, in modern societies appearances and images become predominant and commodities colonize social life; the society becomes a society of the spectacle. The spectacle, as Debord identifies, is "a social relationship between people that is mediated by images"

(p. 12). Harvey (1989a, 1991) argues that capital produces places, built environments, and cities as a spectacle to be consumed by the public. The commodified space of Amman's contemporary megaprojects can be understood as a part of the spectacle that Debord theorizes and Harvey applies to the urban built environment. However, because the term "spectacle" is overused and scholars from different disciplines understand it differently, I find the term "commodified space," as well as the terms "consumption space" and "consumerist space," more appropriate to describe the new megaprojects in the city. The spectacular commodified space of Amman is reminiscent of Gulf cities, reflecting the fact that much of the capital invested in the city's megaprojects came from the Gulf where many urban developments, and cities, had been similarly produced as commodities. Western ideas, images, and consumption patterns shaped and enforced by the logic of capital had influenced Gulf cities' urban developments, which in a city such as Dubai even exceeded developments in Western cities in grandeur, luxury, and consumerism.[5]

Produced for show, Amman's new megaprojects hid the processes and social relations that produced them and became signifiers of attributes such as happiness, healthiness, and eliteness, which the city residents, as well as others, would seek through their consumption of megaprojects. These projects' spectacular buildings and landscapes and upscale shopping, entertainment, residential, and office spaces even turned the city's architecture and landscape into a commodity to be consumed by those who live or work in the megaprojects or visit them. The view of Amman's hilly topography and built environment, as well as life in the city, from these megaprojects became a signifier of gentility that the developers would sell for those seeking social status through the "possession" of this view, thus commodifying the city's landscape. The commodified spaces of contemporary megaprojects promoted a high-end lifestyle based on the significance of the image and upscale commodity consumption. They established new ways and standards of living that many Jordanians could not afford as the new normal lifestyle Jordanians should pursue if they were to join developed societies and achieve the pleasure and contentment modernity promised.

Conclusion and recommendations for future research

This book has sought to understand the influences of Gulf capital flows to Amman on the city's built environment in the early twenty-first century through an in-depth analysis – within a theoretical framework – of three cases of megaprojects launched in the city during this period: The New

Downtown, Jordan Gate, and Sanaya Amman. The book has discussed how Gulf capital inflows intersected with global, regional, national, and local processes, conditions, and agencies – including the circulation of ideas and images, the transfer of expertise, Jordan's modernization project and economic integration, and the agencies of corporations and the state – to transform architecture and urbanism in Amman. This book has argued that recent megaprojects in the city were devised to redefine the identity of the city residents and the nation as modern like their counterparts in the developed world and globally competitive cities and to make Amman a global city. The commonalities these projects exhibited in shape and function with megaprojects in other globalizing cities, particularly in the Gulf, were a means to this end. Unlike the product, the processes that produced Amman's contemporary megaprojects showed some variation on the processes that produced large-scale urban developments in other cities under contemporary globalization. However, the book has concluded that, like megaprojects in other cities competing to maintain or enhance their world status, the new megaprojects in Amman are a part of global capitalism's mode of producing urban space. Furthermore, these developments, and contemporary urban transformation in Amman, cannot be understood in isolation from Gulf capital and its penetration into Jordan's economy, as well as the global economy.

With Amman as its focus, and having investigated the urban built environment against the background of Gulf capital flows and with relation to architecture, urbanism, discourse, and identity, this book provides a valuable interdisciplinary contribution to the scholarly body of knowledge on globalizing cities, especially in the Middle East. This book stimulates further interdisciplinary studies on architecture and urbanism in Amman as well as other regionally and globally integrated Arab cities. In the context of Amman, two important topics relating to the present study are worthy of investigation in the near future.

The first topic is the social impact of Amman's early twenty-first-century megaprojects. The book has shown that these developments affected local communities and social equality in the city. Recent megaprojects in Amman will likely contribute to gentrification in their neighborhoods. In fact, the fieldwork and interviews conducted in the course of this research showed that some negative effects of gentrification had begun by 2010. It is, therefore, recommended that an in-depth study be carried out to explore residents' experience of gentrification as it relates to the new megaprojects in the city.

The second significant topic for future research is the privatization of the public space in Amman and the interruption of social activities, particularly for the less privileged segment of the society, as these relate to the production of recent megaprojects. Of particular significance are the processes through which ownership of property on the sites of these megaprojects was transferred to the developers. The book has addressed these processes and the power relations as well as social implications they involved. However, an extensive investigation of the regulative and legislative processes relating to property ownership and privatization of public space will further our understanding of the multiple dimensions underlying the production of contemporary megaprojects in the city. The future study may address, among other things, voluntary and involuntary selling of privately owned properties, property expropriation, and the roles of the different parties involved in these processes, including the developers, private owners, city officials, and legislators.

Notes

1 GaWC hierarchically ranks world cities under the Alpha, Beta, Gamma, and Sufficiency tiers based on their advanced producer services and integration into the network of world cities. Amman fails to show on GaWC's 1998 list, not even as a city with "minimal evidence" of "World city formation." On the 2000 and 2004 lists, Amman comes under the Sufficiency tier, which includes "cities that are not world cities . . . but they have sufficient services so as not to be overtly dependent on world cities." Amman comes under the Gamma tier on the 2008 list, and ranks higher under this tier on the 2010 list. The Gamma tier cities are world cities that connect small states into the global economy, or significant world cities "whose major global capacity is not in advanced producer services." On the most recent roster (2012), Amman was promoted to a low Beta level city. Cities in the Beta tier are significant world cities "instrumental in linking their region or state into the world economy" ("The World According to GaWC," n.d.).
2 For example, Abu-Dayyeh (2004) traces back the early-twenty-first-century Abdoun Bridge to the elevated roads bridging the city wadis proposed in the mid-twentieth-century plans for Amman.
3 Lu speaks of "the" Western modernity. One can argue that there are many Western modernities, and thus it would have been more accurate to refer to these modernities or to "a" Western modernity.
4 The developers of Sanaya Amman pitched all of these environmentally friendly technologies and designs, which, according to them, would have made Sanaya the first development in the city to be LEED-certified (see Dwairi, 2008; Picow, 2009). Similarly, the Abdali developers and their architects praised the Abdali Mall's green solutions, and they spoke of its natural heating and cooling system and solar panels, emphasizing that this development was designed in conformity with LEED standards to become the first LEED-certified mall in the country (see Associated Press, 2016). The developers also highlighted AID's encouragement of other developers investing in The New Downtown to have their buildings certified by LEED, and they emphasized the gray water system in the project (AID, 2015; Amireh, 2010). However, the Abdali developers were not environmentally conscious when dealing with 750 trees on the site of Phase II of

The New Downtown. The developers proposed cutting down the 80- to 90-year-old trees to implement their designs for the Abdali project. Environmentalists in the city were concerned that the removal of these trees would interrupt the ecosystems they sustain, and these environmentalists as well as others worried that Amman would lose one of the few much needed green areas. Despite recommendation from the Ministry of Agriculture and suggestions from the Farmers Union, environmental societies, and activists that the developers alter the Abdali designs to accommodate the trees, which they argued were a part of the natural heritage, the Cabinet gave AID permission to uproot two-thirds of the trees on the site, requiring that the developers plant in an area outside Amman five trees for each tree they cut (Kraishan, 2013; Namrouqa, 2012).

5 Dubai has become one of the favorite destinations for shoppers not only from the region but also from around the world (see Kapur, 2016). The city has some of the largest malls in the world, such as the Dubai Mall and Mall of the Emirates. Recently, Dubai has revealed plans for what would be the largest shopping center in the world, Mall of the World, which also would have the world's largest indoor theme park (see Cornin, 2014; Fahy, 2015).

References

Abdali Investment and Development (AID). (2015). The New Downtown of Amman. Retrieved March 26, 2016, from http://www.abdali.jo/pdf/abdali-2015.pdf.

Abu-Dayyeh, N. (2004). Persisting vision: Plans for a modern Arab capital, Amman, 1955–2002. *Planning Perspectives, 19*(1), 79–110.

Amireh, G. (2010). Abdali Operations Director, George Amireh, explains why Abdali is an eco-friendly development. *Abdali Newsletter, 10*, 4.

Anderson, B. (2006; first published 1983). *Imagined communities: Reflections on the origin and spread of nationalism* (2nd ed.). London: Verso.

Asfour, K. (2009). Identity in the Arab region: Architects and projects from Egypt, Iraq, Jordan, Saudi Arabia, Kuwait and Qatar. In P. Herrle & S. Schmitz (Eds.), *Constructing identity in contemporary architecture: Case studies from the south* (pp. 151–198). Berlin: LIT.

Associated Press. (2016, July 7). Jordan's newest mall debuts large-scale green technology. *Gulf News*. Retrieved August 4, 2016, from http://gulfnews.com/business/sectors/retail/jordan-s-newest-mall-debuts-large-scale-green-technology-1.1858730.

Barthel, P.-A. (2010). Arab mega-projects: Between the Dubai effect, global crisis, social mobilization and a sustainable shift. *Built Environment, 36*(2), 133–145.

Beynon, J., & Dunkerley, D. (Eds.). (2000). *Globalization: The reader*. New York: Routledge.

Cornin, S. (2014, July 7). Mall of the World: Largest shopping centre on the planet unveiled in Dubai. *The National*. Retrieved July 31, 2016, from http://www.thenational.ae/business/industry-insights/property/mall-of-the-world-largest-shopping-centre-on-the-planet-unveiled-in-dubai.

Daher, R. (2008a). Amman: Disguised genealogy and recent urban restructuring and neoliberal threats. In Y. Elsheshtawy (Ed.), *The evolving Arab city: Tradition, modernity and urban development* (pp. 37–68). New York: Routledge.

Daher, R. (2008b, October). Amman's vanishing legacy of modernity. *Jordan Property*, 10–21.

Debord, G. (1967/1994). *The society of the spectacle* (D. Nicholson-Smith, Trans.). New York: Zone Books.

Donald, J. (1999). *Imagining the modern city*. Minneapolis: University of Minnesota Press.

Dwairi, M. (2008, July 22). Itlaq a'mal al-bina' li abraj Sanaya 'Amman al-sakaniyya bi hajm istithmar 300 million dollar [Launch of construction work on the Sanaya Amman residential towers with an investment size of 300 million dollars; in Arabic]. *Al Rai*, p. 26.

Elsheshtawy, Y. (2004). Redrawing boundaries: Dubai, an emerging global city. In Y. Elsheshtawy (Ed.), *Planning Middle Eastern cities: An urban kaleidoscope in a globalizing world* (pp. 169–199). New York: Routledge.

Elsheshtawy, Y. (2010). *Dubai: Behind an urban spectacle*. New York: Routledge.

Fahy, M. (2015, September 8). Dubai's Mall of the world master plan revamped for transport system. *The National*. Retrieved July 31, 2016, from http://www.thena tional.ae/business/property/dubais-mall-of-the-world-master-plan-revamped-for-transport-system.

Foucault, M. (1969/1972). *The archaeology of knowledge and the discourse on language* (A.M. S. Smith, Trans.). London: Tavistock and New York: Pantheon Books.

Foucault, M. (1984/2003). The ethics of the concern of the self as a practice of freedom. In P. Rabinow & N. Rose (Eds.), *The essential Foucault: Selections from the essential works of Foucault 1954–1984* (pp. 25–42). New York: New Press.

Ghosh, A. (2005, November 19–25). Public-private or a private public? Promised partnership of the Bangalore Agenda Task Force. *Economic and Political Weekly, 40*, 4914–4922.

Harvey, D. (1989a). *The urban experience*. Baltimore: Johns Hopkins University Press.

Harvey, D. (1989b). From managerialism to entrepreneurialism: The transformation in urban governance in late capitalism. *Geografiska Annaler: Series B, Human Geography, 71*(1), 3–17.

Harvey, D. (1990). *The condition of postmodernity: An enquiry into the origins of cultural change*. New York: Blackwell.

Harvey, D. (1991). The urban face of capitalism. In J. F. Hart (Ed.), *Our changing cities* (pp. 51–66). Baltimore and London: Johns Hopkins University Press.

Harvey, D. (1994). The invisible political economy of architectural production. In O. Bouman & R. v. Toorn (Eds.), *The invisible in architecture* (pp. 420–427). London: Academy Editions.

Harvey, D. (2001). The art of rent: Globalization and the commodification of culture. In *Spaces of capital: Towards a critical geography* (pp. 394–411). New York: Routledge.

Harvey, D. (2005). *The new imperialism*. Oxford: Oxford University Press.

Kanna, A. (2011). *Dubai: The city as corporation*. Minneapolis: University of Minnesota Press.

Kapur, V. (2016, May 15). Dubai ranked among world's top 5 hottest shopping destinations. *Emirates 24/7*. Retrieved July 31, 2016, from http://www.emirates247.

com/news/dubai-ranked-among-world-s-top-5-hottest-shopping-destina
tions-2016-05-15-1.630036.

King, A. (1996). Worlds in the city: Manhattan transfer and the ascendance of spectacular space. *Planning Perspectives, 11*(2), 97–114.

Kraishan, M. (2013, January 5). 'Ittihad al-Muzari'in' yujaddid rafdahu li qarar izalat ashjar turathiyya fi al-'Abdali ['Farmers Union' renews its opposition to the decision of removing historic trees at Abdali; in Arabic]. *Ad-Dustour.*

Kubursi, A. (1999). Reconstructing the economy of Lebanon. *Arab Studies Quarterly, 21*(1), 69–95.

Larkin, C. (2010). Remaking Beirut: Contesting memory, space, and the urban imaginary of Lebanese youth. *City & Community, 9*(4), 414–442.

Lu, D. (2011). Introduction: Architecture, modernity and identity in the Third World. In D. Lu (Ed.), *Third World modernism: Architecture, development and identity* (pp. 1–28). New York: Routledge.

Makdisi, S. (1997). Laying claim to Beirut: Urban narrative and spatial identity in the age of Solidere. *Critical Inquiry, 23*(3), 660–705.

Malkawi, S., & Kaddoura, H. (2007). *Ontology of Amman: Soul and body – study of the development of the Arab modern city* [in Arabic with a few sections translated into English]. Amman: Nara.

Massad, J. (2001). *Colonial effects: The making of national identity in Jordan.* New York: Columbia University Press.

Namrouqa, H. (2012, September 18). Activists step up campaign to save trees, landmark from destruction in Abdali project. *The Jordan Times.* Retrieved August 17, 2016, from http://www.siyaha.org/sites/default/files/Press/19 Sep – The Jordan Times – Activists step up campaign to save trees, landmark from destruction in Abdali project.pdf.

Olds, K. (1995). Globalization and the production of new urban spaces: Pacific Rim megaprojects in the late 20th century. *Environment & Planning A, 27*(11), 1713–1743.

Oxford Business Group. (2009). *The report: Jordan 2009.* London: Oxford Business Group.

Picow, M. (2009). Emirate-built Sanaya Amman towers to be Jordan's tallest and first 'green' building. Retrieved August 17, 2016, from http://www.greenprophet. com/2009/06/01/9364/sanaya-towers-jordan-eco-apartment/.

Stallmeyer, J.C. (2011). *Building Bangalore: Architecture and urban transformation in India's Silicon Valley.* New York: Routledge.

The World According to GaWC. (n.d.). Retrieved July 29, 2016, from http://www. lboro.ac.uk/gawc/gawcworlds.html.

Index

Figures are indicated by an *italicized number.*